i need some help here!

HOPE *for* When Your Kids Don't Go according to Plan

Kathi **Lipp**

Revell

a division of Baker Publishing Group
Grand Rapids, Michigan

© 2014 by Kathi Lipp

Published by Revell
a division of Baker Publishing Group
P.O. Box 6287, Grand Rapids, MI 49516-6287
www.revellbooks.com

Printed in the United States of America

Library of Congress Cataloging-in-Publication Data is on file at the Library of Congress, Washington, DC.

ISBN 978-0-8007-2078-0 (pbk.)

Published in association with the literary agency of WordServe Literary Group, Ltd., 10152 S. Knoll Circle, Highlands Ranch, CO 80130.

To protect the privacy of those who have shared their stories with the author, some details and names have been changed.

Manuscript development by Erin MacPherson

14 15 16 17 18 19 20   7 6 5 4 3 2 1

"Kathi has ⸻ ⸻ and impor-
tant couns⸻ is a fantastic
resource f⸻ navigate the
real-life st⸻ ⸻ how life and
kids should go. Kathi has been there, and this wisdom is priceless."

—**Shaunti Feldhahn**, bestselling author of *For Women Only*
and *For Parents Only*

"Our role as parents is to guide our children into adulthood. Our greatest opportunities will often come when they experience various kinds of failures. With grace and truth, Kathi authentically deals with these realities as a mom and stepmom during those not-so-good moments, sharing some great and practical insights and tips."

—**Roy Baldwin**, speaker, popular contributor to Dad Matters
blog, and director of parenting at Focus on the Family

Praise for *Praying God's Word for Your Husband*

"I have concluded that the power and strength of our marriage of thirty-two years come from prayer. I have also discerned that most women feel a little overwhelmed, lost, or confused when it comes to just how to pray for their man. Kathi Lipp tackles this vital issue with practical tips and encouragement, as well as some easy-to-follow prayers, so that every wife can be a praying wife. Husbands around the world, including your own, will be grateful for the fruit of this book as you weave your way through it and apply it with love."

—**Pam Farrel**, author of the bestselling *Men Are Like Waffles,*
Women Are Like Spaghetti and *52 Ways to Wow Your Husband*

Praise for *Praying God's Word for Your Life*

"I recommend this book for anyone needing direction and practical guidance for personal prayer time."

—*CBA Retailers+Resources*

"Kathi Lipp takes us on a life-changing journey to pray God's Word over our lives. I love her practical steps and insights on how to make this a part of our daily routine. Highly recommended."

—**Linda Evans Shepherd**, bestselling author
of *When You Don't Know What to Pray*

Books by Kathi Lipp

Praying God's Word for Your Husband
Praying God's Word for Your Life
I Need Some Help Here!

To Kimberly

*Anyone else might have a problem having a book with this title
dedicated to them, but only you would actually love it.*

*I love you and am so proud of you. God has big things in store
for you, and I love that I get to have a front row seat.*

contents

Acknowledgments   9

Introduction   11

1. Unlikely Gifts   17
2. Don't Hang Out in the Motherhood Alone   27
3. You Are Not the Only One   33
4. When My Child Is Different   51
5. When My Child Is Overwhelmed   65
6. When My Child Is Troubled   77
7. When My Child Is Sick or Injured   91
8. When My Child Makes Poor Choices   103
9. When My Child Is Running Away from God   117
10. When My Child Is Lacking Character   129
11. When My Child Is Struggling   143
12. When My Child Is Left Out   157

Final Thoughts   169
Notes   171

acknowledgments

My biggest thanks go to Erin MacPherson. I can't get over how blessed I am to have you in my life.

To the other "bad moms"—Susy Flory and Cheri Gregory. Not only do you give me support, but you give me tons of material.

And to the team who holds me up—Lynette Furstenburg, Angela Bouma, Kim Nowlin, and Bronwyn Swartz. I am so grateful.

To the kiddos in our lives—Amanda, Jeremy, Justen, and Kimber. Every book there are new stories to share. Thanks for trusting me with yours.

Andrea Doering and the rest of the Revell team. Still shocked and amazed that I get to be with you.

To Rachelle Gardner and the rest of the Books and Such team. I'm honored to be a part of you.

And to Roger, who is the coauthor of all my best adventures.

To each person who has prayed, encouraged, or held us up this year. We are so grateful. God has used you as his hands and feet.

introduction

I feel like I'm failing as a mom.

Please tell me I'm not scarring my kids.

Others joke that they need to save up not for college but for therapy for their kids. I'm afraid that I'm not joking.

As parents, many of us are silently pleading, *I wish someone would just tell me what to do.*

Oh, how often have I heard that same sentence—usually when I'm huddled in a corner, praying with a mom whose child is in trouble. Maybe her daughter is sick or her son has made some bad choices in life. Her toddler is defiant, her teen is running wild, or her adult child is no longer speaking to her. She is heartsick and would do anything—*anything*—to make her child "okay."

When I'm sitting there, my hands clasped around hers, praying that God would change the situation, I don't just feel bad for this poor mom, I feel empathy too. Real, true, deep, heartfelt empathy. Because every prayer we're praying I've prayed a thousand times for my own children:

when my son was asked to leave his preschool class for disruptive behavior

when my stepdaughter said yes to an engagement ring from
the man my husband and I knew was not in God's will for
her life

when my daughter was in the emergency room of our local
hospital for hours on end and the doctors couldn't figure out
why she was having pains that made her scream

when my stepson refused to talk to me at my wedding because
he hated that I was marrying his dad

when I found the medical marijuana card in the laundry

Every single time I thought, *I wish someone would tell me what
to do*. Like you, I want the best for my kids. I would lay down my
life for them. I want to take every pain away, to stop every poten-
tial issue before it happens, to keep them safe and healthy. And I
want them to grow into men and women who love God and live
by his Word.

But, frustratingly, sometimes the next step isn't "do." Sometimes
the next step is to just be still and know that he is God. Yes, the
next step is "pray."

For years I've loved the story of the Amalekite battle in Exodus
17:8–14:

> The Amalekites came and attacked the Israelites at Rephidim. Moses
> said to Joshua, "Choose some of our men and go out to fight the
> Amalekites. Tomorrow I will stand on top of the hill with the staff
> of God in my hands."
>
> So Joshua fought the Amalekites as Moses had ordered, and
> Moses, Aaron and Hur went to the top of the hill. As long as
> Moses held up his hands, the Israelites were winning, but whenever
> he lowered his hands, the Amalekites were winning. When Moses'
> hands grew tired, they took a stone and put it under him and he sat
> on it. Aaron and Hur held his hands up—one on one side, one on
> the other—so that his hands remained steady till sunset. So Joshua
> overcame the Amalekite army with the sword.

Then the Lord said to Moses, "Write this on a scroll as something to be remembered and make sure that Joshua hears it, because I will completely blot out the name of Amalek from under heaven."

I've loved this story for so many reasons:

1. Moses listened to God. He didn't try a bunch of other approaches and then think, *Okay, none of those worked. Maybe I should give God's way a try.* No, he listened to God.

2. Moses was obedient. It shows radical obedience when we're standing in a battle for our own lives.

3. The story shows the power of community. Aaron and Hur are the ones holding up Moses's hands in the battle. When we grow tired and can't keep up the battle, God gives us a model of what real community looks like: supporting each other.

4. The story also shows that comfort is important in these hard times. Not only did Aaron and Hur support Moses's hands, but they also provided a rock for him to sit on. It's not an accident that that detail was included. We don't just need truth in our parenting; we need a community that will love us, pray with us, support us, and believe in us as well.

Recently when I was sitting in church, my pastor, Scott Simmerok, talked about this portion of Scripture. I thought, *I've spoken and written about this Scripture over a hundred times. I could make my shopping list for the week on the back of this church program.* But not wanting anyone to see me ignoring the pastor, I figured I'd better listen and take a few notes.

That's when I realized I'd been missing a huge point in this story all along. Yes, it's about community. Yes, it's about strength and comfort. But the real point?

God won the battle.

It was God. Yes, Moses was obedient. He did what God asked him to do: he stood on the hill with the staff in his hands. He prayed. And when he grew weary, he called in reinforcements.

But it was God who won the battle, God who did the heavy lifting. That is what we as parents must never forget.

We can do so little to effect change in our children's lives. But God can do everything.

When it comes to our kids, we do have someone telling us what to do: Moses. He is a great example. Like Moses, we have to:

1. Listen to God. He has already given us wisdom in his Word.

2. Trust God to win the battle, even when things look dire.

3. Pray fiercely.

4. Do what God says, even if it seems like it won't help.

5. Surround ourselves with people who will provide comfort and strength as we go through the battle.

6. Have patience and allow God to work.

As parents, we must never forget—we can do everything we know how to do.

Recently I was having a conversation with my friend Rob Teigen, who wrote a delightful book called *88 Great Daddy-Daughter Dates*. I was telling him how I've talked to moms about the guilt we have with how our kids did or didn't turn out. Here's the thing: Rob is a great dad and has a bunch of great kids, so I wasn't confident that he would get the angst that some of us parents go through when our kids don't go according to plan. But then Rob surprised me by saying, "I was on a flight a few weeks ago and was talking to a dad who heard I had published a book for dads and daughters, and he was asking me a bunch of questions. He was expressing his disappointment with the fact that he did not have a really close relationship with his daughter. I said to him that I think as parents, we take way too much credit when things go right with our kids and take way too much blame when they go wrong."

We get trapped in the lie that if only we had put our kids in the right school, been there more, and so on, they would have turned out differently. On the other hand, when our child is getting straight

As and leading a missions trip to Mexico, it's easy to take the credit. In both circumstances, we must remember that the battle for our kids is God's.

When we parent, especially when our kids are taking a different route than we expected, it also helps to remember how our heavenly Father parents us.

Author and speaker Michele Cushatt talks about how her thinking changed after going through a prodigal son experience in her own life:

> I used to think of parenting as a math problem. To get extra-good kids, you need to be an extra-good mom. You know, 2 + 2 = 4.
>
> Of course, that was back when I managed every detail of my kids' little lives. Like what they ate for dinner and what time they went to bed. It was easy to think I could control the outcome when my biggest challenge was cutting their meat into itty-bitty pieces.
>
> Then they grew up. And one day our sixteen-year-old left home and refused to come back. Wanting independence and a place free of rules, he rebelled and rejected everything we stood for.
>
> In a moment, my math stopped adding up.
>
> How did this happen? I'd done everything I knew to do, so where had I gone wrong? After years of math, I could make only one conclusion.
>
> It was my fault. Somehow I'd failed at motherhood.
>
> From the moment I became a mother, I'd tried to be perfect, to get it all right. But in all my pushing and striving and expecting perfection, I'd forgotten other key parts of the parenting equation. Humanness. God. And grace.
>
> There's nothing wrong with hard work and striving for excellence. But it's not easy living under the expectation of perfection. In all my efforts of trying to be the best mom (and generate amazing kids), I put too much pressure on myself—and the family. And I missed teaching them about the beauty and covering of God's perfect grace.
>
> Eventually our son came home—repentant, ready for relationship, and one step closer to maturity.

But I too needed to repent. To confess my perfection expectation for both myself and for him. My failures and willingness to own them would've been a much better teacher of the God I wanted my children to know. So I committed to give my children a little extra room to make mistakes, admit them, and come back home. For myself too.

Because, after all, that's exactly what God does for me and you.

So, friends, this book will have a lot of "do." There will be steps to help you deal with not just your kids but your reactions as well. Yes, there will be a lot of "do." But there will also be a lot of "stop," "trust," and "pray." Because as much as you love your kids, they are God's children, and the battle for their hearts, their minds, and their lives is his.

1

unlikely gifts

There she sits across from me—my friend who did everything right as a parent. She and her husband are the "good" parents at church. They have a close, loving family—their kids love and respect them, and they have a strong marriage, serve in the church, and are the first ones anyone calls on when they have a need.

But now she sits across from me. She's a part of the club that no parent ever signs up for.

It's the "Our Kids Weren't Supposed to Turn Out This Way" Club.

Somewhat surprisingly (to me, at least), she and her husband have gone through the initiation that every single member has: realizing her kids aren't as perfect as she thought they were. She's suspicious that her kids are doing one of the things that she hoped they never would.

Whether it's a big thing like drinking, sex, or drugs, or a "starter" crime like lying, sneaking, or cheating, it hurts us parents to watch, especially because often these broken behaviors go much deeper than simple bad behavior. There's also the realization that the behavior has been covered in lies so deep you don't know who or what to trust anymore.

It's the feeling of overwhelming love for your child, but also a rage that cuts to the very core of you as a parent.

I look at my friend who loves her son but is so hurt, is so scared, and feels so betrayed that she is at a loss for what to do, because her kid of all kids wasn't supposed to turn out this way.

I sit and listen to the misdeeds of her son, and while each behavior has ripped to her core, I hear nothing new. Her son has done the exact same things that my kids and most of my friends' kids have done.

Now don't get me wrong. When your kid chooses the wrong way, it causes a lot of undue pain. I tell my friend that. I am careful not to discount or minimize her pain, because I know all too well how bad it hurts to watch a child going down the wrong path. But I also want to reassure her that she is not alone. Not only does she have a God who loves both her and her child desperately and perfectly, but she also has a bunch of prayer warriors and other moms who care enough to pray her through it.

Whether it's a child who is behaving badly, an unexpected illness, or some other issue that has thrown your child off course, it can be devastating. But as odd as it is to say, there are gifts in being the parent of a child who is broken, who is living a life that you never would have chosen for them. There are gifts for you.

So I start the process of inviting my friend into the club. I let her know that through all the pain, the brokenness, the anger, and the tears that seem to break out at the most inappropriate times, there are gifts to being here in this place she never wanted to be.

Here are a few of the gifts that I received through my broken kids—gifts I never would have chosen but am truly grateful for every day.

The Gift of Community

One of the most powerful sentences in the English language is "Me too!" It helps us discover who our people are. You move from sympathy to empathy when you hear that someone is in the same battle you are.

Some of my closest friends started out as acquaintances who, once their children went off the rails, became my mom army. My closest comrades in arms.

Sometimes it's hard to find those other parents. We have all become so good at building our kids up that it feels like a betrayal of our own when we admit that things are not all lollipops and unicorns in our little corner of the world.

But other moms who have "been there, done that" are worth seeking out. They are worth opening up to. They are the ones who are going to tell you, "Yep, this may be the hardest thing you ever go through. Yes, this is painful, but you are going to get through it. You have a new normal. But you will be okay." And then at some point you get to say that to someone else. You will feel less alone. When your kids are having problems, it can lead to isolation, but once you get past the point of feeling like it is only happening to you, you will find your people.

And when you find your people, make sure some of them know your God. You need to be reminded in the hardest times that God loves you and God loves your child. It's easy to forget that, so you need people who have walked this way before to point you the right way—back to God.

The Gift of Authenticity

Here is the text I received this morning from a church friend I met with yesterday: "I feel compelled to encourage you to somehow include in your book that the major reason I called to talk to you about Marcus is because you have been so honest and transparent about your own life."

Ah, the gift of authenticity.

Oh, how I kept pushing this gift back across the table to God. I didn't want people to know my struggles. I didn't want them to see the messy stuff, the mistakes, the moments of distrust, the wrong decisions. I didn't want them to think I was a bad mom.

But I found that whenever the Holy Spirit was prompting me to share my story with someone, whenever I was authentic about my struggle as a parent, I was rewarded. Maybe it was a chance to encourage another parent, or I was the one on the receiving end of encouragement. Maybe there was a piece of advice I desperately needed, or there was a connection to an expert or another parent who could help us through.

There are, of course, some people you shouldn't share with. There are some people who feel that if only you had done everything right, your child wouldn't have problems. These people usually fall into three categories: those who have never had kids and think they could do better, parents who have one child under the age of three and think that the same principles of discipline apply to teens, and parents of children over age thirty who have blocked out all the bad years.

Pay attention to the voice that says, "Go ahead, trust." Then be transparent and share your heart.

The Gift of Usefulness

I feel plenty useful in my everyday life. I cook meals for my family, I walk my dog, I write books, and I pray for a lot of people.

But something is different when you have a broken child and you are able to clear a path for another broken parent.

Have you ever been to one of those team-building retreats? I have. And it felt like a colossal waste of time. We did trust exercises, breathing exercises, the whole bit.

Yawn.

That is, until we got to one exercise. The prize? A $100 gift certificate to Starbucks.

When they announced that, I thought, *Okay, things just got interesting.*

What did we have to do? Get to the end of a trail before the rest of the team.

I'm not known for being super quick on my feet. So I self-selected out of this competition and kissed that coffee good-bye.

Linda, the woman in charge of the whole retreat, started to announce the rules. "I have set up a trail somewhere on these campgrounds that you will need to find and complete, using the clues I put in your envelope along with any one item from this room." Her hand swept across the space, gesturing to all the tools at our disposal—a map of the campgrounds, a compass, a flashlight, flares, a pickax (!)—whatever we found helpful.

Everyone scattered with their envelopes and tools and headed out to find the trail.

As I was waiting for the room to clear, I went up to Linda and asked, "I can take anything from this room to help me?"

With a sly smile, she nodded. She knew exactly what I was going to do.

I grabbed Linda's hand and said, "Show me the way." So she did. And that Starbucks gift card was mine.

There is a special gift in being able to say, "I've been there. I'll show you the way."

Your new friend—the one who just found out that her baby girl is smoking pot—may have some friends she can share her pain with, but most will not understand. Yet perhaps you've been there. You have the souvenir mug. You can be someone to her that no one else may be able to—her guide in the forest as she tries to get to the other end.

To some of you, my kids' problems contained in these pages may seem mild compared to the devastation some families go through. So when I asked my friend, speaker Jill Davis, to share the story of her son's drug addiction, I questioned if she would be able to find the "gifts" in such a heartbreaking time in her life. Here is what Jill had to share:

"Mom, guess what I did today?"

I had heard these words hundreds of times during my son's life. From snakes to kittens to skinned knees and broken hearts, I thought no answer would surprise me. But nothing had prepared me for what he said: "I tried opium."

David was my impulsive, loving, second child. At seventeen, he had just come out of a difficult eighteen months, which included depression and multiple suicide attempts. He was in therapy, and I really believed we were through the worst of life and headed for smooth sailing. In actuality, we were just headed into the storm. David had always been an overachiever and quickly went from trying pot to being a heroin addict in about two weeks.

Opium was not a word in my vocabulary, and I had to google it to find the meaning. What I found was that David had actually tried heroin that day. Heroin comes from opium. My kid was a heroin addict. This was outside the realm of possibility in my reality.

I was the good mom, the supermom. I was respected and often asked to teach parenting classes. I trusted God's guidance for each of my children. I had dedicated David to God before his birth. I named him after the David of old, as I wanted him to become a man after God's own heart.

We lived in a nice neighborhood, and I had done everything a good mom was supposed to do. I had homeschooled, studied learning styles, become an expert on positive reinforcement, taken my children to Sunday school and vacation Bible school, and tried to be obedient to my church's teaching on parenting.

I read every article and book possible on child rearing. I worked hard to apply the skills I learned. I was prepared to be mother of the year with high-achieving kids. I was not prepared to have an addicted child. I was angry with God and felt betrayed by David's addiction to heroin.

I felt more lost and alone than I had ever felt in my life. I was already in a crisis of faith due to my divorce, and now God felt distant and I was bitter toward him. There was no warm fuzzy feeling that God would take care of everything or that "in all things God works for the good of those who love him" (Rom. 8:28). The God of my faith had abandoned me.

I had lost much of my faith community after my divorce, but I had not lost faith that God was present in my life. Until I had a friend look at me and say, "What did you do wrong for David to become a heroin addict?" I looked around my small group and realized that question was on the face of almost every woman there. I said I had not looked at him the first time I held him in my arms and thought, *I hope he grows up to be a heroin addict.*

I left the church and didn't go back. No one from my small group or my church ever contacted me.

My crisis of faith was no longer. I simply had no faith. I lay in bed and cried. I drove my other kids to school and cried. I went to work and cried. I had done what God had asked of me, and now I had a kid who was a heroin addict.

There was no book out there called *Raising the Heroin-Addicted Child.* At this time there was no small group for "good" moms raising an addict. I had been abandoned by my friends, my family, and now my faith.

Yet deep in my soul I felt I was not alone. My tears and pain became part of my path back to faith.

As I was driving home one day, trying to decide on the next step, the song "Blessed Be Your Name" started playing. The lyrics encouraged me to sing praises no matter if I was in a place of abundance or in a forsaken place.

I knew this was my answer back to faith. I began to let go of the pain of abandonment by my friends and my community of faith. I began to acknowledge my bitterness toward God. I began to let go—slowly—of my anger at my son for being an addict. I began to be grateful for all that was around me. Gratitude was my way of singing praises. Each day became easier.

David was still an addict, I was still without my friends, and my previous understanding of God had changed forever. It would be four years of addiction and rehab until David was no longer a using heroin addict.

My friends didn't come back, parenting didn't become easier, and I didn't feel immediately closer to God. Yet in this place of pain and sadness, I learned to walk in gratitude.

I still remain in this place of gratitude. Each day is a gift, and God is in everything around me. I will be grateful.

Gifts from David's Addiction

Gift: a thing given willingly to someone without payment; a present.

When I think of David's addiction and the gifts that came with it, I do not see it as something without payment. I paid highly for the gifts. I lost friendships, lost family relationships, lost income, lost time, and experienced many other great losses.

What I gained, however, was much greater than any of these losses.

Gift 1: I learned true grace.

Throughout my lifetime I thought I knew the meaning of grace. I believed in the grace of God, and I offered my children and friends grace. I even named my daughter Grace because she was an unmerited gift from God.

However, even as I lived in what I thought was grace, there were always times of judgment. I judged when I saw a mother with unruly children—I would think, *She needs to get her kids under control. I am a better mother than her.* I judged when I saw a Christian couple get a divorce—I would think they just didn't work hard enough. I judged when people did not live up to the standards I had subconsciously placed on the world.

When the judgment was turned on me, I realized that the expression "but for the grace of God go I" was not truth. I went where I went with God's grace following me as I parented an addicted child. His grace sustained me throughout. In actuality, it was because of God's grace, there go I.

Now when I see someone struggling or not meeting the arbitrary standards set by others, I remember the phrase "Be kind, for everyone you meet is fighting a great battle." This kindness to all is true grace.

Gift 2: I learned faith.

I grew up and lived in a faith system that was all about rules and shame when the rules were broken. Struggling with having an addicted child and watching David struggle with his addiction, I realized that God was present in all places. No matter what.

He was present when I didn't get all the rules right. He was present when others shunned me. He was present through every single loss. Even when my crisis of faith took me down a path where I believed God did not exist, he was present.

I learned that faith is much more than a list of rules to follow and the hope of getting into heaven. Faith is about believing in the divine—a God who provides unconditional love in all situations. These days instead of having a shaky faith, I have an unshakable faith in God's love and forgiveness.

Gift 3: I learned to forgive myself.

When I saw all the judgment around me and felt criticism for being the parent of an addicted child, I felt such great guilt. What had I done wrong? Why had my child turned out this way? What was wrong with my parenting skills? And on and on I beat myself up.

I finally realized that I had done the best I could with what I had from where I was in life, and it really was good enough. I now can forgive myself for both the big and the small mistakes I have made and that I continue to make. I have asked my children to forgive me for what I have done wrong. I was not a perfect mom, but I was the mom God chose for them, and therefore I was the perfect mom for them.

This is the road no one wants to travel—the road of having a child that is struggling. But there are priceless treasures along the way if you allow God to work in your life and your child's.

I'm sorry if you have these problems. Really, I am. In this book, I am going to talk a lot about how to have peace in the midst of these very difficult circumstances. But I also want to reassure you that you will learn things along the way. When you are broken-hearted, you are broken open for other people to see into you and see what they need. When you are brokenhearted, God can do so much more with you than with the one who thinks they have this whole parenting thing down. You are teachable. You are humbled. You are attentive to the workings of God in your life and the lives of your kids.

And this, my friend, is a priceless gift.

2

don't hang out
in the motherhood alone

My journey to motherhood didn't start out like I had planned it. (Shocking that my plans didn't involve a before-marriage pregnancy or having to work two jobs to pay for diapers). And things didn't exactly improve from there. After two kids, two stepkids, three trips to the ER, four failed classes, six nasty teenage/young adult breakups, and a massive fight at the mall (where complete strangers questioned my ability to parent), I've learned one thing for certain: kids never go as planned.

And this is a good thing.

Not to get all sentimental on you, but had my kids gone exactly the way I had planned, they wouldn't be the strong, independent, insightful, and creative adults they've grown up to be. Nope. Instead, they'd be mini-me's, complete with a Starbucks addiction and a love of sappy novels.

And you know what? The world isn't big enough for a gaggle of Kathis. Or Rogers. Or anyone elses. That and the line at Starbucks is long enough already.

I'm going to tell you this right up front just so we're all on the same page: I know that your kids will not always do things the way you would want them to. Your toddler will throw tantrums. Your preschooler will be defiant. Your preteen will be disrespectful. Your teenager will throw tantrums (yes, sadly, we circle back to that). And mine have too. It's pretty much a motherhood guarantee: your kid will break your heart.

But I have another guarantee for you. Once your heart has been broken for your kids, God can use that brokenness to woo you to be the kind of parent he needs you to be. Not only can God take those broken pieces and turn them into a heart that beats for him, but he can also use the pieces of broken promises, unfulfilled expectations, and sin-destroyed lives. You just must be willing to hand them over to him. He will do the hard work of restoration for you because you are his child. And if anyone understands the fierce love of a parent, it's him.

Yet those brokenhearted times are very lonely for a parent. God is the only one we can completely rely on for all of our parenting needs. But I'm convinced more than ever that each of us needs a few God-appointed women in our lives to survive this thing called motherhood.

Over a year ago, I finally opened up about my struggles with my kids to a couple of trusted friends. It was a scary thing to do (would they think less of me? Would they feel I'm a fraud?), but I knew that if I kept everything between just my husband and me, either I was going to explode or my marriage was.

Two of the people I confided in? Erin MacPherson and Cheri Gregory.

Erin is one of those moms who looks perfect from a distance, but if you spend more than thirty-five seconds with her, she'll let you know that she's bribed her kids with money and treats, she's hidden in the bathroom longer than a socially acceptable amount of time, and on some days she would rather hang out with her dog than her kids. She's an amazing mom, and part of the reason she's an amazing mom is because she is an honest mom. She loves her preschool-aged kids more than life itself but admits frequently that it's hard to be a mom.

Cheri and I have already swapped some parenting war stories, as we have kids that are about the same ages and stages (college and young adults). Cheri is one of the most intentional moms I've ever met. She loves her kids and cares deeply about their character, their unique personalities, and their relationship with God.

I've asked each of these fellow moms in the trenches to share some of their mom stories in the following pages. Erin writes what she learned about parenting from watching her own parents deal with her struggles as a not-so-perfect child, and Cheri writes for all you moms who are in the "been there, done that" stage of parenting and still want to have a godly influence over your grown-up kids.

We're going to be real. We're going to be honest. And if we're so transparent that you think we're bad moms, well, we've beat you to it. We've all felt like that. In fact, a few of us have formed a club.

The Bad Moms Club

When I was opening up to Cheri about some of the things I was feeling, we decided we needed a place to support each other, love on each other, pray for each other, and remind each other that we loved our kids even when they weren't being very lovely.

We called ourselves the Bad Moms Club.

And then we added another member, Susy Flory. Another "good mom" who was on the dark side of parenting.

For over a year, we have shared the joys, sorrows, triumphs, and God-movings of our families with each other.

Why are we called the Bad Moms Club? Our name is twofold:

1. We have labeled ourselves "bad moms" for so long because of some of the choices our kids have made. It was a name we felt deep in our bones but never dared to whisper since someone could find us out. We were finally able to say, loudly and safely, "I feel like a bad mom!"

2. Part of the reason we banded together is that we needed the prayers and strength of other moms as we told our kids "no" much more loudly, much more clearly. We had to become the "bad mom" to our kids. The ones who wouldn't rescue our kids from their poor choices. The ones who wouldn't put our own lives on hold because our kids had a whim to go to the movies or to a friend's house. The ones who wouldn't have debit cards at the ready to loan them money they chose not to earn. We are also sometimes known as the "mean moms."

The three of us have seen each other through some of the most difficult parenting challenges I can imagine. The whole time, we've felt like bad moms—guilty, out of control, ashamed, terrified. But the beauty of our little fellowship is that we are able to speak truth into each other's lives. We can hold each other up with God's Word, prayer, and reminders of the boundaries that we know are best for us—and best for our kids.

Brené Brown, in her book *The Gifts of Imperfection*, defines compassion this way: "I felt totally exposed and completely loved and accepted at the same time."[1]

That is who Cheri and Susy are for me. They have seen me at my worst—all of it—and loved and accepted me (and my kids) at every step.

My friend Karen recounted a time when she was having an issue with her husband. It was over something small (dishes? laundry?), but at the time it was a huge deal. She spoke with a friend about how to get herself and her husband on the same page.

Karen's friend started to go on and on about how Karen's husband was inconsiderate, self-involved, and just a bad guy.

Karen was mortified. Here this woman was degrading her husband. Karen loved her husband. Yes, they had issues, but she was on her husband's side.

A loving and compassionate group of friends will let you talk about your troubles without bashing those you are struggling with. They will empathize and sympathize, but they are always looking for and praying for the best for you, your marriage, and your relationship with your kids.

I've heard the stress, anxiety, and worry that Susy's and Cheri's kids have put them through, but I can honestly say I love those kids more today than when we started this group a year ago. I hardly know them (we all live pretty far apart and rarely hang out in person), but I've grown to know and love them through their moms. I have compassion for my friends and their kids.

I know that Cheri and Susy know things about my kids that could cause them to jump to my defense and take my side when it comes to our issues. But Susy and Cheri are not on my side. They are on the side of God and my family.

The three of us choose to separate each other's children from their behaviors. Our kids can be truly lovable without the lovely behaviors.

Uncover the tribe of women God has given you. I honestly believe that you do not need to go out and find these women to bring into your life. Most of us have these people right around us. There are other moms who are in the same stage of parenting you are. Those who will get it and love you anyway.

Or maybe the moms are online. If you have a child with a specific challenge, you need to be around other moms who understand it. There are online support groups for every kind of issue. A great place to start looking for support is the (in)courage website, www.incourage.me.

Finally, pray for these women! I'll be honest, I didn't pray that God would find me two friends I could dump my troubles on. I did pray that God would comfort me in my pain, and he's the one who sent Susy and Cheri. Prayer isn't answered in the way we expect, but God knew what I needed more than I did. He sent me an army.

3

you are not the only one

When I started writing this book, I asked my Facebook friends (Hi! And thank you!) the following question: "Can you tell me what area of parenting is the hardest for you? I know for me, it has always been follow-through in setting boundaries and committing to consequences. What is it for you? Are you too strict, too lenient? Is it time? Is it worry? There is no shame in admitting our struggles."

When I asked the question, I honestly thought most moms would talk about a part of parenting where they and their child were struggling. But as the responses piled up, I noticed several trends starting to develop:

guilt
control
worry
shame
more guilt

The issues that were hardest for moms really weren't about the kids at all. They were about the *feelings* moms had about their parenting.

As moms, we face all kinds of trials, and each of us has a different burden to carry. But regardless of whether you have a high-energy toddler or a defiant teenager, you probably feel guilty, worried, controlling, and even ashamed about how you parent sometimes. And after reading all of those heartfelt responses, I felt like I couldn't move forward with this book until I addressed the way our kids' behaviors make us feel as moms.

When Moms Feel Guilty

If only . . .

I hadn't worked when my kids were little

I had worked when my kids were little

I hadn't gotten pregnant so young

I hadn't waited as long to get pregnant

I'd been more patient like my friend So-and-So

we had unplugged the TV

we'd eaten all organic

we'd had more family time

we'd saved more for college

I'd breast-fed longer

Oh, the "if only" list could go on forever. (And you could probably make your own list to rival anyone's out there.)

When my son Justen was three years old, I needed to go back to work part-time and had to find a babysitter for him. I interviewed a number of people and finally settled on a sweet grandma who was watching her own grandson. While I knew this was a great situation, I had a lot of mom guilt about leaving Justen. How was he going to get along without me? Would he spend hours crying for me after I dropped him off? Would he feel abandoned? All those thoughts raced through my head as I dropped him off with lots of hugs, kisses, and his favorite "boo banky" (blue blankie).

As he ran to play with the other little boy, I lingered at the door for just a moment or two. I was so relieved that Justen was transitioning well into his new environment. I looked at him all glassy-eyed, waiting for the tears to start, and then . . .

"Mommy. It's time for you to go."

What? I was being asked to leave by my own son.

A new flood of guilt washed over me. Had I not done enough to bond with Justen? How could he walk away so easily? What had I done wrong as a mom?

And so it goes: the mommy guilt dance. Even when I got the result that I wanted (i.e., Justen didn't throw a fit when I left), I still found something to feel guilty about.

How is it that we can find a reason to feel guilty no matter what the situation?

Whether it's dropping your child off at a babysitter or dropping them off seemingly unprepared for the world of college, we will find a way to feel guilty about it.

The Reasons We Feel Guilty

Most of our guilt seems to come in four varieties: we feel guilty because we didn't know any better, because we knew better but did it anyway, because we compare ourselves to other moms, or because our emotions don't seem to be very mom-like.

We Didn't Know Any Better

One mom accidentally transferred the oil from a jalapeno to her son's skin while changing his diaper. I locked my baby in the car and had to wait an excruciating forty minutes for the auto club to arrive. Mistakes happen. But it's easy to still feel guilty even though we had no intention of hurting our child, physically or emotionally.

We Knew Better But Did It Anyway

Let's face it: sometimes these kids just *wear you out.* Your kid has asked to stay up late for the hundredth time. You've resisted. You've held your ground. You've sent her back to her room eight times after she's come out for a drink of water or she heard a noise. Like a military intelligence operative, your child knows your weak spots and has worn you down. You let the terrorist win, and now she's sitting on the couch watching *House Hunters* with you two hours past her bedtime. And tomorrow? You're going to pay for it with a grumpy child and an extra load of guilt.

We aren't always going to make the "right" decisions. Sometimes it's easier to cut ourselves a break and do something easy.

Things like Nintendo as a babysitter and Happy Meals come to mind.

We Compare Ourselves to Other Moms

Other moms can be one of our greatest sources of strength or our greatest guilt inducers. It all depends on how we are feeling about our own mothering and on the moms we are hanging out with.

Several years ago, I showed up at church and everyone (or at least it felt that way) had a Louis Vuitton handbag.

I'd never really noticed all those LV bags before, but suddenly I became obsessed with getting my hands on one. I talked about which size and style of bag I wanted, which of my kids I was willing to trade for it, and all the ways that it would be so practical and useful for me.

The fact that the bag I wanted was the price of a down payment for a house didn't seem to enter into my reality.

I knew the bag was out of my reach financially, so I thought all of my friends from church were just better at handling money.

I went around dejected for a while until I asked my friend Dina about it. How did she afford such an expensive bag?

"Kathi," Dina said, "it's not a Louis Vuitton—it's a Phooey Vuitton. It's a knockoff. I bought it out of the back of some guy's car."

With handbags and with mothering, we tend to do the same thing: we compare our reality with someone else's fantasy, and we always come out lacking.

Make sure you're hanging out with other moms who are keeping it real so you don't end up comparing the reality of your family to someone else's fantasy.

We Have Un-Mom-Like Emotions

A friend of mine told me last week that at that moment, she kinda, sorta hated her son. Then she quickly recanted what she said and gushed on and on about how much she adored her kid . . . but I knew the feeling.

Let's be honest: there are times in all of our lives that we don't like our kids much. And that's okay. If you really think about it, I bet there are times that God feels the same way about us. There have been times in my life when I'm sure God was looking down and saying, "That Kathi! She just doesn't learn! She makes the same mistakes over and over and over." But you know what? Even when I'm royally screwing up, God still loves me. And the same goes for your kids. You can love your kids fiercely and still not like the ridiculous things they are doing at any moment.

I love this quote by bell hooks (intentionally lowercased) and think it fits exactly with where we—the moms of troubled kids who are doing troubling things—need to be: "To begin by always thinking of love as an action rather than a feeling is one way in which anyone using the word in this manner automatically assumes accountability and responsibility."[2]

I can love my child with boundaries, prayer, and grace even though I don't always feel loving toward them. It is my actions rather than my feelings that qualify me as a loving mother.

Fighting Mom Guilt

Increase your self-compassion. I've had to do it hundreds of times.

Say that a friend has had a bad mom moment. Her child swallowed something of a nonfood nature and she had to call poison control. She yelled, got mad, and locked herself in her bedroom.

How do I respond? With compassion. "We all have bad days," I say soothingly. I give her a graceful way to know that she is still loved, still valued, and still a good mom.

But what if I'm the mom who had to dial 911, or I said something to my kids that I swore I would never, ever say? I will wallow in my own muck and mire for days.

Yet self-compassion tells us to have the same mercy on ourselves that we would have on our friends. Self-compassion says that our value is not wrapped up in our parenting that day.

Also, understand who loves you. I think it breaks God's heart to hear how we talk to ourselves—without grace, without mercy. God is not surprised by our failures, but it must be so disheartening to him when we become judge and jury for ourselves. Remember that God loves you passionately and wholly.

When Moms Feel Out of Control

Our younger cat, Ashley, never does anything the easy way.

We feed her. Religiously. In fact, every morning and every evening, my husband or I fill the cat food bowl to the tip-top. We make sure there is more than enough to feed the cats for three or four days, because otherwise we have two angry kitties body-slamming our bedroom door in the middle of the night to let us know that the staff has fallen down in their service and this need must be attended to immediately. (This happens even if they still have food in the bowl but can see any spot of silver at the bottom of the bowl. Just the thought of running out of food makes them destructive.)

So it's a complete puzzle to me as to why Ashley feels the need to break into the food supply any chance she gets. And we're not talking an open bag of kibble sitting in the corner of the kitchen. We have a country-style dish hutch in the dining area of our kitchen. It has open shelving on top and closed shelves with sliding doors on the bottom, where we store all the animal food. The hutch is painted a yummy tomato-red everywhere except the edge on one of those bottom doors, because that is where Ashley has spent hours—and I do mean hours—trying to nudge, scratch, and force that door open.

Once she finally opens the door, which weighs as much as she does, she proceeds to crawl into the hutch, find the bag of cat food, then claw and nibble at the bag until the cat food pours out all over the shelf of the hutch. Not the first thing you want to wake up to in the morning.

The thing that boggles my mind is that the food she spends all night trying to get to and damaging furniture to get to is the very same food that we pour into her bowl every morning and every evening of her life. So here is my question: why is Ashley working so hard and destroying things along the way when she has never wanted for a single piece of kibble a day in her life?

And now I wonder: have you ever had similar thoughts about your own kids?

Maybe it's your child who does his homework but then fails to turn it in when he gets to school. Maybe it's your adult child who is helped by anxiety medication but refuses to take it. Maybe it's your daughter who is pursued by a wonderful, upstanding, godly young man but chooses instead to date the unemployed marijuana smoker.

You scream inside your head, *Why do you have to make everything so much harder than it needs to be? Why do you keep messing up?*

I wonder if some of us go into parenting hoping for a do-over. We know the mistakes we've made, and now we have the chance to make things right. We can learn from our past, and this time, with this tiny person, we have the opportunity to make things better.

At least that's what I thought before I gave birth.

Maybe you had the same vague idea before you had that baby or adopted: *Finally, this is my chance to get it right.* And now, like me, you're laughing at your former, non-parent self because you've come to realize you just don't have that much control.

The loss of control is one of the hardest things to deal with as a parent. When our kids are little, we get to choose so much for them: the clothes they wear, the friends they hang out with, the food they eat. But as they get older, our control over them decreases as their independence increases, and that's a scary thing. As much as we want to box them in, bind them up, put them in padding, and manage their every decision, that control starts to slip away.

For many of us, it's the first time we send them off to school—preschool, kindergarten, or college—that the loss of control hits us the hardest. Or maybe it's the time your child brings home a friend that you can just tell is going to be the one sitting next to your kid the first time you get a call from the principal, asking you to come into the office.

For some of us who are divorced, it's the first time you send your child over to the other parent's home. You have no control over who your kids are staying with or what they are exposed to.

And not only does that wreak havoc with our kids, but it messes with us as well.

The Monkey and the Coconut

In high school, my teacher told the story (which turned out to be a legend) of how scientists in Africa humanely caught monkeys for research. The scientists would drill two holes into a coconut—one just big enough to pull a string through, and one just big enough for a monkey to slide its hand through. Once the coconut was tied to the tree, the scientist would put a piece of fruit in the coconut. When the monkey came along, it would reach into the coconut for the piece of fruit. But as soon as it made a fist to grab the sweet treasure, it no longer could pull its hand out of the coconut through the small hole. So the monkey would sit there, refusing to give up the piece of fruit, for up to two days.

As a high schooler, all I kept thinking was, *Stupid monkey. How could you give up your freedom to hang on to one little piece of fruit?*

But now, as a parent, I truly understand giving up your freedom to hang on to the thing that you so desperately want but can't have.

My friend Cheri knows about the tendency to overinvest in our kids' outcomes. Here is what she had to share:

One day last fall, I noticed on Facebook that a friend of my daughter had posted photos of a recent event at their college. I clicked on the link, thinking it would be fun to look at photos of my alma mater.

The pictures were taken at the school's fall festival and showed students playing games, eating food, and socializing. All sorts of fond memories came flooding back, especially since my husband, Daniel, and I met during our freshman year of college.

And then I clicked on a photo that caused me to freeze in alarm. At first all I could see was an arm—an arm absolutely covered with tattoos.

Please know: this story is not about tattoos; it is about what God taught me through my reaction to them. I have always had a visceral reaction to tattoos, and on that day I was dismayed by what looked to me like black and green and red bruises.

But that was nothing compared to the desperate horror I felt when I looked up the arm to the face and recognized my own daughter.

My stomach twisted into a knot, and I felt like throwing up.

I thought, *Daniel is going to kill her, then me . . . or maybe me first and then her. He is going to hit the roof.* I could feel myself wanting to hide in a closet already, just thinking about his reaction.

And then I was hit with a wave of shame. *What will people say about us? Other faculty members at the school have children who become student missionaries, and I have a daughter who gets tattoos? What will the students say? What does this say about us as parents? As teachers? I should quit! We should move!*

41

And then fury: *Those cost money. A lot of money. Here I am returning clothes I need so that I can pay for her textbooks. Of all the ungrateful, entitled, self-centered . . .*

I wanted to take action. Text her, email her, call her, drive up to the college and put her in the car and drive her to a tattoo removal clinic. I wanted to *let her have it.* This was too much. This was not just over the line, this was far above and beyond *anything . . .*

I'd been having a perfectly nice, normal day until I saw that photo. And suddenly I was in the midst of a situation I did not need. A situation I did not ask for. A situation I never dreamed I'd ever have to deal with.

As desperate as I felt about the tattoos, I was more desperate not to let my own reaction hurt my daughter or harm our relationship. I was very upset, but I knew if my reaction came out in the wrong way at the wrong time, it would be so powerful that it could do untold damage. I wanted to protect my daughter from myself, and I wanted to protect our relationship. This meant I had to deal with my stuff on my own.

So the one thing I did "right" was the hardest thing I know how to do: nothing.

For several months, I did nothing about her tattoos. Oh, I did a ton of work processing my reaction to her tattoos! But I did nothing that directly involved my daughter.

I headed to the Bad Moms Club, where Suzy and Kathi sympathized and held me up in prayer. They told me that they would feel the same way I did, which was such a relief. I saw my counselor and was encouraged to hear that she felt my reactions were not judgmental, not unloving, not close-minded, but well within normal for a parent who had just been completely blindsided. I spent several months reaching out to my support system and hunkering down in my prayer chair, taking care of myself. So when the time came to talk with my daughter about her tattoos, I was equipped to choose my words and tone with care.

The loss of control is so very, very hard. That is a common theme throughout this book. We move from control to influence in our child's life, and those changes can feel like little deaths.

But like the monkey, we have to give up our prize—our little illusion of control—in order to have the bigger prize. Our freedom.

When Moms Feel Worried

Worry was the trait that most women listed as the one that makes them feel like the monkey in the story, holding on to things they should let go of. They worried about their kids' education, health, future spouse, and salvation.

Now imagine your child co-piloting a small plane across the United States.

That's what Cheri had to endure. She was a natural worrier, and this was more than a poor mama's heart could stand:

> My son, Jonathon, was born early and spent his first week of life in the NICU.
>
> I still remember how frightened I was when they whisked him away from me after I gave birth. How tiny and fragile he seemed in the incubator.
>
> We were so relieved as he grew to be a healthy toddler. One night as I kissed him good night, he accused me, saying, "Mama! You had chocolate!" I tried to convince him, "No, I had carrots!" But he was positive: "Mama, you smell like chocolate!" Even though he had busted me, I was so thrilled that all his senses were working just fine!
>
> When Jonathon was a senior in high school, he took private pilot ground school, and an amazing opportunity opened up for him. He was invited to help fly a private plane from Milwaukee, Wisconsin, to Monterey, California. For just the cost of a one-way ticket to Milwaukee, he would gain invaluable experience and flight time.
>
> We didn't have much time to think about it. Jonathon decided to do it, I purchased the ticket, and Daniel drove him to San Francisco International Airport.
>
> When Daniel returned from the airport alone, I started to panic. With Jonathon out of my motherly reach, I freaked out. I began to feel as if I'd put a tiny baby on a plane to Milwaukee.

I didn't even know where Milwaukee was, and looking at a map didn't help in the least—he was practically on the other side of the country from California!

I decided to calm myself by looking up information about the plane. Seeing the Tinker-Toys-and-duct-tape contraption (with a zipper instead of a door) that was referred to as a "light aircraft" only inflamed my fears.

Jonathon was supposed to be home in three or four days. But due to bad weather, his trip stretched to nine days. By day two, I wasn't eating. By day four, I wasn't sleeping.

I sought sympathy from some of the men at church, but they expressed nothing but envy: "Oh, I wish I was on that plane!" Not one of them understood the agony I felt, wondering where my baby was, how he was doing, whether he was safe.

My compounded worries felt so true that I was shocked when my "baby" emerged from the plane standing six feet tall and sporting a scruffy beard.

His big smile and first hug was for Mom. But it wasn't until going through photos taken right after his landing that I noticed something huge that I completely missed at the time. In one photo, Jonathon is shaking hands with Jay Ketelsen, our school's vice principal of operations and a licensed pilot. And this photo shows something happening that does not include Mom.

Jonathon was a helpless baby when I birthed him into this world. He was a boy when he started his trip from Milwaukee to Monterey. But he emerged from that Tinker-Toys-and-duct-tape plane a transformed person. In the photo, not only is Jay welcoming Jonathon back home; he is also welcoming him into the world of men.

All my worries about my son were valid—at one point in time. Many, many years ago. And that's the problem with the worries I keep nurturing long after they've outlived their usefulness. They feel so real, so immediate, so true.

I'm more of a situational worrier. I don't worry about my kids much on a global level, but if they come home three minutes after curfew, my mind can go to wild and exotic scenarios that include

international kidnappings and ransom notes for deutsche marks.
So I asked Cheri (whose alter ego is "Anxiety Girl") to give us some
practical steps to combat worry:

1. **Pray.** "Pray without ceasing" takes on all new meaning when
   you're under attack from worry. Some days you may need
   to whisper, "Lord, I give this concern to you" over and over.
   You may add a little variety with, "Lord, I give *this* concern
   to you," and "Lord, I give this concern to you *again.*"

   Do not worry (!) that God will tire of hearing the same
   thing over and over. He is delighted each and every time you
   turn to him rather than give in to worry.

2. **Breathe.** Take a deep breath in and hold it; exhale slowly
   and hold it. You can do this as a breath prayer, praying,
   "Your Word to me" as you breathe in, "Your work in me"
   as you hold; "Your strength through me" as you exhale, and
   "My need of you" as you hold. Conscious slow breathing
   disengages your body's fight-or-flight system by sending
   relaxation signals that counter worry reflexes.

3. **Replace worry with God's Word.** Collect a core group of Bible
   verses that speak directly to you in the midst of your worry.
   Memorize them or put them on carry-along cards. Make them
   your go-to thoughts when worry starts trying to hijack your
   mind and emotions. You can also paraphrase them so you can
   recite them in the first person: "I will be strong and courageous. I will not be afraid; I will not be discouraged, for the
   Lord my God will be with me wherever I go" (see Josh. 1:9).

4. **Aim for a 5:1 ratio.** According to marriage researcher John
   Gottman, healthy marriages have a 5:1 ratio of positive com-
   munication to negative. When couples who are struggling
   make an effort to increase their positive interactions, their
   marriages improve.

   This ratio isn't limited to marriage. When you find yourself battling worry, you can consciously dilute the impact of

it by intentionally thinking and verbalizing positives. Compliment the pastor's wife on her new dress. Thank your child for helping with the dishes. Call a friend and invite her for coffee. Worry will recede as you actively focus on what's good in your life.

5. **Review your gratitude journal.** If you're not keeping a gratitude journal, start one. Grab a piece of paper and jot down three things you're grateful for right now. (You can buy the fancy journal later and glue the paper in it!) After a week or two, challenge yourself to write five things a day. Then ten. Keep it near you throughout the day or return to it morning and evening.

    Once you have several hundred things recorded, your gratitude journal will become a concrete record of God's faithfulness in your life despite the circumstances. When worry tries to take over, you can open your journal and say, "See here? And here? And here? No way, worry—you lose; God wins!"

When Moms Feel Ashamed

When I was in my early twenties, one of the ways I tried to earn money was to be an in-home consultant with a now-defunct rubber stamp company. I loved sales and I loved teaching, so it was a natural fit for me. One fascinating aspect of this job was going into other people's homes to throw parties where everyone could come, make a card, and have the opportunity to purchase stamps, inks, glitter, and paper punches.

One woman throwing a party—let's call her Terry—called me up in advance to let me know the rules of her home.

Yep—rules for me coming to her house.

Rule #1: We were only going to use stamps with a God theme—Scripture, prayers, and so on.

Rule #2: Nothing to do with Halloween or any other non-Christian holiday. (Fourth of July? Out. New Year's Day? Out.)

Rule #3: No birthday stamps.

Rule #4: No romance. No "love" stamps, nothing that was flirty. It was weird.

I kind of understood what was going on—she was part of a very conservative group of people I had hosted other parties for, and she was the grand master of making sure that nothing she or her family did, said, or participated in could be considered anything but totally within the bounds of her worldview.

I distinctly remember thinking, *What an exhausting way to live.* But hey, who was I to judge? This was a woman who homeschooled three of her four kids (she had a sixteen-year-old, a fourteen-year-old, a ten-year-old, and a newborn), was a leader at their church, and ruled her group of homeschooling friends with an iron fist.

When I arrived at their home with my newly assembled "Jesus stamping kit" in tow, I started to set up. The whole family minus the dad was there, including the sixteen year-old's boyfriend. The daughter and her boyfriend were taking turns holding the newborn while he slept, and I thought, *What an amazing family.*

Then the baby got fussy. As the daughter was bouncing and trying to soothe the infant, she finally announced, "I'm going to feed him." She and her boyfriend went to the back of the house to feed the baby.

It didn't strike me as weird until I realized—they didn't bring a bottle with them. Hmm. How was the baby's sister going to feed him without a bottle?

And just about then, the guests started to arrive.

I got the party started. We made pretty little cards. Everyone was happy and chatting. It was getting off to a good start.

And then the daughter and her boyfriend came out with the baby.

Everyone was oohing and aahing over this new little life. And everyone was thrilled to see the sixteen-year-old—apparently it had been months since anyone had seen her.

And now it was all coming together. The baby wasn't the mom's; the baby was the daughter's.

This family had gone to such extravagant lengths to hide their daughter's "mistake" that they were now pretending that the mom had had the baby instead of the daughter.

Wow.

I'm not shocked that the daughter had a baby at sixteen. I was pregnant and unmarried myself. It's not a route I recommend, but it's clearly something that happens—a lot.

What was so shocking was the extensive cover-up this family had gone through in order to hide the pregnancy.

Later on I found out it was well-known among their friends that the baby was the sixteen-year-old's, but none of them dared say anything and break down the myth of the perfect family.

Now, let's be clear—I have done the shame game myself many, many times.

I ignored that my daughter's eyes were bloodshot after she spent the night at a friend's. I loaned my son money when he didn't have any to go hang out with his friends. I failed to mention to my mother-in-law that my daughter's new roommate was her boyfriend.

All out of shame. All out of fear that someone would point and call us out for being bad parents.

Shame is a prison we build from the inside out. We gather the bricks and start constructing the walls to protect ourselves—a lie here, a half-truth there—until we realize that it's just easier to pretend everything is okay. To pretend we are fine. And the easiest way for us to pretend is to not have anyone ask any questions, so we hide out. We drop contact with people who care and are asking questions. We isolate ourselves from life so we can protect ourselves and our kids.

And then we find out we are all alone in the shame prison. That there is no longer anyone to reach out to.

Now, sometimes our kids are lying to protect us, especially when they are young.

And then there is the other, twisted side of their lies and behavior—sometimes our kids are banking on our shame to keep their secrets.

Sometimes our kids want to lead a double life:

Be one thing at home and another at school.

Be a partier with their school friends but a Bible study leader at church.

Live with their girlfriend but not tell their grandparents.

And some of our kids are expecting us to fall into place with their double lives. They think, *My parents would never let me fail in high school, because that would shoot down their dreams of college for me.* Or, *My parents won't talk about me sleeping with my girlfriend because they don't want to be known as "those kinds of parents."*

And if we buy in, we just keep building that wall.

My husband, Roger, and I recently had dinner with our friend Keith. Keith and his wife, Rachelle, have two sons, Mike and Chad. Keith and Rachelle are one of the most Christ-committed couples we know. They have both had some rough patches in life, but they have come out digging deeper into God.

Keith and Rachelle were excited about Chad's new girlfriend, Kirstin. She came from a great family, and Keith and Rachelle would often hang out with the kids and Kirstin's parents. What an extra blessing—to like not only your son's girlfriend but her family as well.

So of course they were extremely disappointed to find out that Chad and his girlfriend had decided to move in together.

Suddenly the big family get-togethers were a thing of the past. Why? Because Chad and Kirstin didn't want Kirstin's parents to find out about their new living arrangements.

When Keith and Chad had a discussion about it, Keith was very clear. "We are not going to lie for you. We are not going to cover this up. You are making adult decisions, and it's not up to us to be a part of your cover-up. And another thing? Kirstin's parents know. They may be putting their heads in the sand so they don't have to confirm that they know, but they know."

It is not your job as a parent to cover up for your child. I'm not saying you have to talk about your child's marijuana use in every conversation, but I am saying that you don't have to live in shame because of what your child is doing.

When you tell people, some are going to be shocked. But most are going to know what you're going through or have someone in their lives who is going through something similar.

When you live in shame, you are giving your kids power to dictate your emotions and feelings in that situation.

Covering up for your child leaves you in a place where you have to become double-minded. And that is not how God wants you to live.

4

when my child is different

I have an unnaturally strong reaction to those bumper stickers that say "My child is a star student at Such-and-Such School!" And let's be clear: my reaction is not a positive one.

From day one of his kindergarten class, I kind of figured that my son Justen was never going to be bestowed with one of those stickers. He was the kid that drove good teachers to seriously consider becoming air traffic controllers so they would have less stress in their lives. Justen was the kid who was slouched in his desk chair, reading a book, tapping his leg, and playing with a rubber band all at the same time. He just couldn't sit still.

So when a teacher would call on him, hoping to catch him not paying attention, it was doubly infuriating that Justen always knew the answer. Apparently he could multitask: distract the entire classroom while concentrating on whatever the teacher was saying at the same time.

But not my Kimberly. She was the child who sat in the front row with hands folded, raised her hand to be called on, and looked for ways to help the teacher out. She did her work without being bribed or nagged and got along with the other kids in her class. (Okay, she did have a couple of report cards that said, "Kimberly tends to share with her neighbor while the teacher is talking." But, hey, the girl comes by it honestly. Look at who her mom is.)

When Kimberly started school, I knew that bumper sticker was finally going to be mine. (Wait, did I say mine? I meant hers. . . .) I figured by the end of September, we would be proudly sporting that sticker on the back of the minivan.

But every other week the school assembly would take place, and every time Kimberly came home empty-handed. Weeks turned into months, and by the time we got to the end of the school year, Kimberly was the only one in her class who hadn't received a sticker. The only one.

Now, even though it was a big deal to me, I never mentioned the sticker to Kimberly. Not once. But Kimber was smart. She knew that she was the only one who hadn't received a sticker.

When I asked the teacher about it (because you know I had to), she simply explained, "Well, Kimberly already is well-behaved. There was no incentive to give her a bumper sticker."

If your mommy heart is anything like mine, it is breaking right now even if you've never met Kimberly. (Mine still breaks, and this was more than ten years ago).

I think one of the most painful things we can go through as a parent is seeing an area where our child is left out—whether it's due to a social dynamic, being differently abled mentally or physically, or some other area—where they are missing out on something important or feel like they are not quite good enough to get something they want or even deserve.

Maybe your child is lacking in some key area, whether it be physical, emotional, financial, or social. Maybe there is a sport that your child loves but doesn't have the physical prowess to do well in. Or there is a group of kids at school who have chosen to leave your child out. Or you have a child with a disability, and no matter how hard you as a parent work to make sure they have access to everything they want, they still face situations where it's obvious they're different.

When My Child Is Different, I Feel Desperate

For a few years I was a single mom and my kids and I were broke. In comparison not with the truly impoverished in our world but with the kids around them, my kids were definitely in a different tax bracket, and it showed. They could feel the difference, and I longed to make that feeling go away for them.

I hated that they had to go without. It hurt my heart to tell them they couldn't go to the school trips, church activities, and movies with their friends that they wanted. Every parent wants to give their child good things.

No mom wants her kid to be different for any reason. So I started to feel desperate.

And when I feel desperate, I try to make things happen.

I applied for every job I could find, even some that felt a little iffy (a payday loan officer, for instance—yep, I was desperate). I fell behind on my bills because I wanted to give my kids not only what they needed but what they wanted.

It's natural to want to give your kids what you can, but when it starts to interfere with how God wants you to provide for them, you run into problems. And at that time in my life, I ran into problems.

I started cutting corners—skimping on my church tithe, not giving to people I knew were in need, and starting to feel fearful when any mention of money came up. And I have to tell you, in having that experience, I can kind of relate to the feelings of the man in Numbers 15 who was trying to provide for his family by gathering wood on the Sabbath:

> While the Israelites were in the wilderness, a man was found gathering wood on the Sabbath day. Those who found him gathering wood brought him to Moses and Aaron and the whole assembly,

and they kept him in custody, because it was not clear what should be done to him. Then the LORD said to Moses, "The man must die. The whole assembly must stone him outside the camp." So the assembly took him outside the camp and stoned him to death, as the LORD commanded Moses. (Num. 15:32–36)

Stoning seems a bit severe, I admit, especially when it comes to working on the Sabbath, but the fact was this man was not trusting God, even though God had come through so many times before. He decided he needed to provide for himself and his family by gathering wood on the Sabbath. Yes, God took care of all of their needs, but he felt he needed to take matters into his own hands.

I have been there. It happens again and again. I can't see a way to provide for my family, or if God is working on it, he's taking his own sweet time, so I take matters into my own hands. Like the man in Numbers, I hustle. I work when I should be spending time with my family, I skip the payment plans, I do what I think needs to be done instead of trusting God and his faithfulness.

So when I get into that place of hustling, how do I remember to trust God instead of relying on my own capabilities? God commanded a unique reminder for the Israelites:

The LORD said to Moses, "Speak to the Israelites and say to them: 'Throughout the generations to come you are to make tassels on the corners of your garments, with a blue cord on each tassel. You will have these tassels to look at and so you will remember all the commands of the LORD, that you may obey them and not prostitute yourselves by chasing after the lusts of your own hearts and eyes. Then you will remember to obey all my commands and will be consecrated to your God. I am the LORD your God, who brought you out of Egypt to be your God. I am the LORD your God.'" (Num. 15:37–41)

Blue tassels. God wanted them to make blue tassels to remind themselves to follow God and not go after what they thought they wanted.

As a parent, I need to resist the urge to go after what I think my kids need—an easier time on the soccer field, an easier time at school, different friends, the clothes they want, they shoes they covet—and pray that we would all develop a heart for what God wants for us. That's the only way that we will ever be truly provided for.

I have blue tassels all over my house. I put them up as a reminder that my first job is to stop hustling and start trusting.

When My Child Is Different, I Feel Desperate, but God Is my Provider

> And my God will meet all your needs according to the riches of his glory in Christ Jesus. (Phil. 4:19)

The Bible is chock-full of stories where God miraculously and lovingly provides for his children.

I think one of the most well-known stories in the Bible is when Jesus feeds a crowd of thousands with the food from one little boy's lunch. It's in John 6:5–13 if you want to look it up, but the gist of the story is that Jesus took a little boy's Lunchable and turned it into a feast for thousands of people.

It's a seemingly simple Sunday school story with powerful implications: God will take care of his children when they are different . . . anything. If you feel lacking in any area, whether it's friendship, confidence, hope, or even a shiny "My kid is an A+ student" bumper sticker, God is your provider.

There is a catch: God always provides for his children in the way that's best for them, but it's not always in the way they want. Think about Rachel, Jacob's favored wife in the Bible (Gen. 29–30). She had everything—she was beautiful and desired and loved. But she wanted a son. When God gave her a son, she immediately started asking for another one. As we see in the story, her second son actually led to her death (Gen. 35:16–19). God doesn't always provide for us in the ways we want, and when he does, it can be a double-edged sword.

If I look back at Kimberly's first grade experience, I realize that God never gave me (ahem, I mean, my sweet Kimberly) a bumper sticker, but he did give her a teacher the next year who was able to build her confidence in a way that was lasting. And he gave me a heartfelt lesson in how he supplies exactly what his children need when they need it.

I am just going to come right out and say it: we are all different. None of us have the smartness, savviness, faithfulness, or goodness to be enough. But God is our provider, and he gives us all that we need to be what he wants us to be. Many times that means less money, less opportunity, less something than we think we need.

And so, when my kids are different, my prayers have changed from "Help them to be enough" to "Be their enough." Here are some examples of how that looks.

A Story from the Trenches

We had always dreamed of having the perfect child. As I propped my swollen feet on the coffee table, my hubby would nuzzle in beside me, audibly imagining the perfection that would come neatly wrapped in our firstborn, the world's first perfect child. It was the least we could do, really, to share our perfection with the rest of the world!

That is, until the call came from the doctor that things might not be quite so perfect. One amniocentesis and two weeks later, the results were in. Our little guy had one extra chromosome and Down syndrome.

Down syndrome. The weight of those words fell on my chest like a coat of armor. As I gasped for the next breath, my mind raced. *How can this be? I love God and serve him! Why would he allow this? How will I ever be enough for this child? I have no idea how to do this! They say that God gives special children to special people, but right now I wish God had chosen someone else. I don't want to be this kind of special!*

The news of our son's disability sent us over the emotional edge and left us questioning everything we thought we knew. James 1:17 tells us, "Every good and perfect gift is from above, coming down from the Father of the heavenly lights, who does not change like shifting shadows." *Perfect.* So what about our little guy, with an extra chromosome that would forever blemish his ability to grow and learn? *Perfect?*

Oh, the tears! The hurt, the pain, the fear. But as Christ followers, we have the luxury of the Holy Spirit inside of us. He served as our comforter and our counselor. Somehow, through God's enabling, we decided to live beyond our throbbing emotions, take God at his word, and believe that this gift, though different, was impeccably perfect. In faith, before ever laying eyes on our little wonder, we chose to name him Jonathan. The name means "Jehovah gave."

We had to grieve the loss of the child we thought we would have so that we could fully embrace the perfect gift God had chosen for us all along. Nineteen years later, I am still learning how to squeeze out frantic prayers in the midst of this challenge-filled assignment. But the blessings? Gracious, the blessings that this good and perfect gift brings into our daily lives are innumerable. In the words of the great theologian Buzz Lightyear, the list of blessings from our son Jonathan goes "to infinity and beyond!"

Some of the specific gifts I receive as Jonathan's mom are:

1. **The gift of laughter.** Nothing thrills my Jonathan more than making his mama laugh, so he seeks giggle opportunities on a minute-by-minute basis. He pretends to march in the color guard when putting the shopping cart back in the return caddy at the supermarket. In the swimming pool, he has perfected a stealth underwater swim, making a tunnel out of my legs so I will flip over and gurgle! And oh, how about the time that he found a "present" that the doggie left on the carpet and snuck it under my pillow as a surprise?

2. **The gift of perspective.** Jonathan's goals in life are limited. They usually involve chickenfriesandcoke (yes, all one word to him) and plenty of leisurely living. He is not encumbered by deadlines and is 100 percent unaffected by the opinions of others.

3. **The gift of the sacred.** Much like a person who is sight impaired develops a keen sense of hearing, my mentally impaired son, I am convinced, has developed a keen sense of spirit. Completely sensitive to the moving of his maker, he understands God in a way that I may never fully comprehend. Just the other day, I glanced at my rearview mirror and saw Jonathan in the backseat. He was holding his fast food meal box toward heaven, muttering something under his breath. After several minutes had passed, he put the box down, lifted a hand toward heaven, gave God a knowing wink, and enjoyed his food.

When you know that your child is different—they are missing something that other kids have—it can be the greatest struggle, the greatest disappointment with God we can go through. Without the relentless pursuit of God in our lives, without going to his throne every single day and asking him to help us see the gift of this child, we are going to miss out.

Melodie Griffin

I love Melodie's honesty when she says, "We had to grieve the loss of the child we thought we would have so that we could fully embrace the perfect gift God had chosen for us all along." We all have dreams for our child, and as long as we cling to those dreams, we are going to miss out on the gift that our child is sitting right in front of us.

Practical Steps

It's easy to feel desperate for our children—especially when they are different in a way that we think needs to be changed. I remember feeling so desperate for my Kimberly after the aforementioned bumper sticker incident. I was desperate for her to have something—anything—to show her that she was a good student. My mind started to whir as I thought about how I could go to the mall and get a custom-printed sticker just for Kimberly. Or maybe a certificate that I could print off of Print Shop (yes, we had that back in the day). Or maybe I could get a trophy made? But then it dawned on me that I was trying to take matters into my own hands and be Kimberly's provider instead of letting God be.

The truth is that I will never be able to be my kid's true provider. But God can be. Here's how you can help your kids when they are different:

1. **Allow God to heal desperation.** *God will provide. God will provide.* Say it with me. *He. Will. Provide.* When you feel desperate for your kids, start praying that God will replace your desperation with a sense of peace, of truth, of hope.

2. **Go to Scripture.** I already said this once, but let me reiterate: the Bible is full of examples where God miraculously intervenes for his children in big and powerful ways. And God will not hesitate to do the same for your kid. One thing I've done when I'm feeling desperate about something is to look up stories about how God provides for his people. Just type the word *provide* into the keyword search on biblegateway.com and you'll find more than a hundred results that talk about times that God provided for those he loved. Read them and be reassured.

3. **Don't try to be a do-it-yourself provider.** Remember that story about the Print Shop certificate I tried to make? Admit it: you laughed when you read that. Our human efforts at providing when our kids are different will always fall short. Now, I'm not saying that you should just stop cooking dinner and assume God will provide (oh, but wouldn't that be nice sometimes?),

but when you're feeling desperate because your kid is different, turn in prayer to the one who can always provide.

4. **Champion your child selectively.** I did think it was appropriate to ask Kimberly's teacher about the sticker, but when I got a bad answer, I had two choices: take it up the ladder or pray for Kimberly, my heart, and the teacher. I finally (after a lot of stewing) took the second option. I still don't think the teacher's decision was fair (and how hard would it have been to come up with one more sticker?), but instead of being surprised every time my child is not given what they want, I need to reframe that incident as an opportunity for my child (and myself) to lean into God.

   There are times to champion our children and times to let our child ask for what they need. I want to step in when my child is not able to do so for herself. If my child forgets her homework, it's not up to me to fight the teacher's rules—my child needs to take the zero and hopefully learn for the next time. But when it comes to getting my child with learning challenges the help he needs in the classroom, stand back and watch this mama bear roar!

5. **Champion your child's gifts.** When your kids are different, it's easy to focus on those differences. But reminding yourself—and your kids—of their gifts on a regular basis is a great way to combat that lacking feeling you may be carrying around on behalf of your children.

6. **Don't expect God's answers to be your answers.** It's easy to start thinking that our answers are the right answers. Before you assume you know exactly what your kids want and need in life, remember that God's ways aren't our ways. And even if you think you've figured out a way to, say, extend the school year an extra week so your daughter can get her one chance at a bumper sticker, remember that God is working behind the scenes to provide for your kids in a way that transcends all understanding.

7. **Help your child find their tribe.** There are groups where your child will be part of the team. Find those groups. Give your child a place to belong.

. . . . .

Prayers for My Child

Now he who supplies seed to the sower and bread for food will also supply and increase your store of seed and will enlarge the harvest of your righteousness. You will be enriched in every way so that you can be generous on every occasion, and through us your generosity will result in thanksgiving to God. (2 Cor. 9:10–11)

Lord God, you have promised again and again to provide for us through your incredible righteousness. Thank you for your generosity! I thank you for giving my kids everything they need, and I pray that you continue to pour down your provision upon them so they can grow and thrive and become the men and women you envision them to be.

Trust in the LORD with all your heart
and lean not on your own understanding. (Prov. 3:5)

Alpha and Omega, you are everything we need in this world. Help me not to lean on my own understanding but instead to trust you with everything I do. I give my children to you—especially when they are different. Provide for them in ways I cannot imagine.

His divine power has given us everything we need for a godly life through our knowledge of him who called us by his own glory and goodness. Through these he has given us his very great and precious promises, so that through them you may participate in the divine nature, having escaped the corruption in the world caused by evil desires. (2 Pet. 1:3–4)

Father God, my great provider, you have given me everything I need to live a full and godly life. Likewise, you have given my precious kids all they need so they're never lacking in this world. Lord, pour your glory and goodness on them, and allow each of your great and precious promises to be fulfilled in their lives. I pray that this world—including my own human nature—will never turn them away from the glory to which you have called them.

* * * * *

Prayers for Me

You will again have compassion on us;
    you will tread our sins underfoot
    and hurl all our iniquities into the depths of the sea.
        (Mic. 7:19)

Lord, I know it's only through your great compassion that I find myself fulfilled. Thank you for tossing away my iniquities so I can be given your great grace.

Look at the birds of the air; they do not sow or reap or store away in barns, and yet your heavenly Father feeds them. Are you not much more valuable than they? (Matt. 6:26)

Jesus, you are the great provider. You take care of each member of your kingdom with generosity. Lord, when I am lacking, fill me with the confidence to know you will miraculously and powerfully provide. Remove the desperation I feel when I am not enough and replace it with the ability to fully hope and trust in you.

In all this you greatly rejoice, though now for a little while you may have had to suffer grief in all kinds of trials. These have come so that the proven genuineness of your faith—of greater worth than gold, which perishes even though refined by fire—may result in praise, glory and honor when Jesus Christ is revealed. Though you have not seen him, you love him; and even though you do not see him now, you believe in him and are filled with an inexpressible and glorious joy, for you are receiving the end result of your faith, the salvation of your souls. (1 Pet. 1:6–9)

Lord, I rejoice in your provision! Even though this world sometimes feels unfair and unhopeful, I know that I am never lacking because I have you. I love you, Lord, and I pray that every day on this earth, you will refine me so I can love you, trust you, and hope in you even more.

5

when my child is overwhelmed

June 14, 1976, was a terrible, horrible, no good, very bad day for the fourth grader who is now Kathi Lipp. It was the last day of school and my birthday, and I had chicken pox. Being the social creature I am, I was heartbroken that I was missing the last day of being with my friends. And as I was sitting on our couch, itching and scratching, my bike—my snazzy purple glitter bike with the big banana seat and purple and pink streamers on the handlebars—got stolen. Happy birthday to me!

My parents felt so terrible about it that they went all out to make the evening better: We went to the drive-in that night (so I wouldn't infect anyone outside of the family—and let's admit it, I looked scarier than any monster from a B horror flick) and brought Chinese takeout in the car. They let me and my little brother eat it with chopsticks, so by the end of the night there were tiny pieces of fried rice and chow mein all over the car. And no one said a word about the mess because all they wanted to do was to make sure my very bad day became a kind of bad day by the time I went to bed.

My point? Your kid is going to have bad days. Things will happen—big and small—that will cause your kid's emotions to go haywire. These bad days may be truly justified—a bad grade, a blip in the school play, a fight with a friend. Or it could simply be that Sally got an orange fruit snack and your kid just got an orange. Regardless, your kid's emotions are real and painful. And as a parent, you have to surround them with all the love, hugs, prayers, and Chinese takeout they need to get through.

When My Child Is Overwhelmed, I Feel Powerless

Bad days—heck, bad weeks—happen. Even for adults. But when it happens to a kid, it kind of makes our mama bear hearts want to sob. That story I told you about my last day of fourth grade? It was pretty rough for me. When my mom and I talked about what had happened, I broke down into hiccuping sobs.

But my mom knew just what to do. She didn't laugh or dismiss me or tell me it would be okay. Instead, she took me into her arms and simply let me be. She didn't try to control things, to fix things, to solve things; she just let me cry, let me talk, and let me know I was loved and cared for and supported regardless of my bad day. Then she did everything in her power to turn that day around. And you know what? She succeeded. When I look back on that day, I don't get teary or emotional because my bike got stolen or because I missed the last day of fourth grade. I get teary and emotional because I remember feeling heard, cared about, and ultimately loved.

As moms, it's easy to try to control things when our kids are struggling. To call up that big mean girl's mom and talk to her about what's going on. Or to call the school to find out what happened, how to fix it, how to make it better. Sometimes that's the right thing to do. But we don't get to be with our kids 24-7. And we don't get to fix all of their problems. On that day in fourth grade, my mom could no more make my beloved bike reappear than she could keep me from getting chicken pox. I'm sure she felt powerless. And the truth is that she was. But God wasn't.

When My Child Is Overwhelmed, I Feel Powerless, but God Is in Control

I will cry to God Most High,
To God who accomplishes all things for me. (Ps. 57:2 NASB)

If I could tell you only one thing that I've learned as a mom, I'd tell you that no matter how much your kid is struggling and no matter how out of control you feel, God is always in control.

One of my all-time favorite verses is from one of the most read and memorized sections of the Bible, 2 Corinthians 4. I'm sure you probably know it, but go ahead and reread it a few times and really let Paul's words sink in:

> But we have this treasure in jars of clay to show that this all-surpassing power is from God and not from us. We are hard pressed on every side, but not crushed; perplexed, but not in despair; persecuted, but not abandoned; struck down, but not destroyed. We always carry around in our body the death of Jesus, so that the life of Jesus may also be revealed in our body. For we who are alive are always being given over to death for Jesus' sake, so that his life may also be revealed in our mortal body. So then, death is at work in us, but life is at work in you. (2 Cor. 4:7–12)

Everything we have in this world—our joy, our happiness, our struggles, our pain—is fleeting. But regardless of where we are—hard-pressed, crushed, perplexed, persecuted—we are never, ever abandoned. Go ahead. Read the verses again. Roll them in your heart. Think about the implications: When our kids struggle, they are not in control. When our kids struggle, we are not in control. When our kids struggle, the God and Creator of the world—the author of life and the giver of abundance—is in complete and total control and is working behind the scenes to put all things together for good.

For us moms, this stuff is hard. Especially as we're sitting there with our kids falling apart. It's easy to forget that God cares for us and our children. But that's why it is so vital in these really hard places to remind ourselves that in the hurting spots, God cares more than we can ever know.

A Story from the Trenches

I was sixteen.

My dad had just had surgery and my mom was at home taking care of him, but my newfound ability to drive meant that my social life didn't have to miss a beat even though my parents were laid up. And so the night after my dad's surgery, I bade my parents adios and gave them the house to themselves.

I hopped in their little red Ford Escort (yes, it was very, very cool) and headed to Young Life. Afterward, my boyfriend and I decided to get frozen yogurt before heading home to do homework. Wild night on the town, it was.

It turned out to be. As I turned out of the parking lot, a big-wheeled truck backed into the lot to turn around. The truck struck me on the driver's side door, crushing the left side of my tiny car under its too-high bumper. My boyfriend, in his own car, hurried over to make sure I was okay. I was.

I was stunned. But my boyfriend took charge. He helped me out of the passenger side, took down the other driver's insurance info, and talked to him while I stood there in a daze, staring at the car my dad loved. I was in a bit of pain—nothing serious. But the car—the car my sick-in-bed daddy had scraped together hard-earned cash to buy—was absolutely crushed. I was heartsick. How was I going to tell my parents?

I stood in front of the pay phone (we didn't have cell phones back then) for twenty minutes with quarters in my hand, hemming and hawing about making the call. Finally I picked up the phone. Tearfully, I told my dad what had happened, choking back sobs as I told him the car—his car—was ruined.

It was twenty years ago, but just thinking about that conversation makes me get choked up. My daddy handled the situation with so much grace. My tears were met with comfort. My confessions were met with, "It's okay." My fear was met with reassurance. My worry for him was met with genuine concern for me. I was comforted with a reminder that God is always in control. And my bad day turned into a day when I knew without a doubt that no matter what happened—no matter how bad a day I had—my daddy would still love me.

Erin MacPherson

Practical Steps

How does a mom go about reassuring, comforting, and loving her kids through a time of struggle? Here are my tips:

1. **Pray quietly.** Grab that sweet, emotional kid of yours into a big bear hug, and as you rub her back, pray fiercely. Pray that God would fill her with a spirit of hope. That he would soothe her soul. That he would intervene and help her to find the peace that transcends all understanding.

2. **Don't preach.** Remember that time you started sobbing while you were cooking dinner because after you added a dash of salt your sauce got too salty, and dinner dissolved into a tear-fueled mess? And remember how your husband intervened and tried to give you all sorts of advice that only made you cry harder because he knows nothing about your sauce, and all you wanted was a shoulder to cry on? Yeah. That. Sometimes your kids don't need advice or suggestions, they just want a shoulder to cry on. Next time your kid comes home an emotional mess, try biting your tongue and just be

with your kid. Let him talk. Let her cry. Listen. Hug. Listen. Repeat.

3. **Don't minimize.** If your biggest problem was that Sally and Jane didn't want to sit by you at the lunch table, then your life would be going pretty well. Yes, your kid's problems are just that: kid problems. I get that they aren't big bad adult problems, but that's a good thing. Your kid has her whole life to deal with those! For now, do your best not to minimize her emotions or feelings—because while the things she's upset about may not be big to you, they are to her.

4. **Don't judge.** It's easy to adopt an "I would never have done that" attitude with your kids—especially when they do and say things that are, well, ridiculous. Yes, your kids sometimes make—shall I say it?—dumb choices. Yes, what they did might have contributed to their problems in some way. But save pointing that out for a day when they are feeling a bit less emotional. And even if you would've never (ever ever) borrowed your mom's shirt and spilled cafeteria ketchup on it, that doesn't mean you wouldn't have done something equally inconsiderate. So try not to judge your kid's choices (even if you think they were downright ridiculous), and instead allow natural consequences to be the best teachers.

5. **Have a real conversation . . . later.** I already said that on your kid's worst days, probably the best thing you can do is listen, love, and listen some more. But that doesn't mean your kid doesn't need to learn and grow from what happened. Wait a few days and then take your kid out for slushies and have a real live mom-to-kid conversation. Tell him about some of your worst days and what you learned from them, and let him vent about what happened to him.

Most of these are "don't," not "do." And "don't" can be really hard for a parent. It's so much easier if I ask you to do something for your child ("Go bake your kids some brownies") than if I ask you not to do something ("Don't tell them that this will blow over"). No one is giving out blue ribbons for the mom who is biting her tongue. But know that every time you "don't," you are doing the deep, hard, God-breathed stuff that is growing you and your kids.

Probably your best approach is to model for your child what it looks like to be okay. Kids need to see a model of what it's like to have emotions without allowing them to be the basis for bad behavior or justification for outbursts. Our kids need to see what it looks like to be mad, sad, and frustrated, and still be okay. Here is author Cheri Gregory's process of becoming a mom who models being okay:

> Annemarie flings her paintbrush down in frustration. "I just can't get this right!"
>
> I glance at her painting, start to open my mouth to tell her how nice it looks to me, and then stop myself. *You don't have to make everything okay*, I remind myself.
>
> "I know I get frustrated when I'm writing a blog post and my words aren't flowing," I say, trying to empathize.
>
> Annemarie's next sigh borders on anger.
>
> *Well, that didn't help*, I scold myself. I start to feel the familiar tightening in my stomach and neck.
>
> *You don't have to absorb her feelings. You don't have to be upset just because she's upset. She doesn't have to be happy so that you can be happy. She can be upset and you can be happy.*
>
> I sigh and consciously relax my muscles, slow my breathing, and recite my morning Scripture.

A Mom Who Makes Everything Okay

I never intended to be a meddling mom. As a teacher, I've complained loudly about hovering "helicopter parents" who stunt their children's maturity by doing everything for them.

However, I failed to see that each time I jumped in to "rescue" my kids from upsetting situations, I was teaching them that they needed everything around them to be okay before they could be okay internally.

What a dangerous lesson!

If you'd asked me, "Cheri, do you want your child's sense of self to be dependent on her external circumstances?" I would have assured you, "No way! That's a terrible way to live!"

But during their growing-up years, my children heard me vent about all the people problems that blindsided me, complain about irresponsible students and critical parents, blame my bad evening mood on everything that happened to me during the day, and yell at inanimate objects such as traffic lights and computer screens.

Looking back, I see that I modeled for my children how to be overwhelmed by circumstances beyond their control.

Which is a nice way of saying that I raised them to be victims.

A Mom Who Models How to Be Okay

I spent so much time, energy, and money desperately "making everything okay" for my kids when they were little. How I wish I'd invested instead in learning how to "make me okay" *despite* everything.

Rather than a mom who modeled how to be overwhelmed, I could have been a mom who modeled how to be okay.

But today's morning Scripture gives me hope that it's never too late: "May the God of hope fill you with all joy and peace as you trust in him, so that you may overflow with hope by the power of the Holy Spirit" (Rom. 15:13).

Trusting God to Work Things Out for Your Child

"This looks stupid!" Annemarie shouts.

All joy and peace . . .

"I'm no good at watercolor. I have no patience!" She is near tears.

. . . as you trust in him . . .

Oh, how I want to do something—anything—to make everything okay!

. . . you may overflow with hope . . .

But I know I can't. And I'm finally learning—some twenty years late, but hopefully better late than never!—I shouldn't even try. . . . *by the power of the Holy Spirit.*

Cheri Gregory

● ● ● ● ●

Prayers for My Child

I have told you these things, so that in me you may have peace. In this world you will have trouble. But take heart! I have overcome the world. (John 16:33)

Lord, you are bigger and stronger than all the troubles in the world! What reassurance that gives me on my toughest days. I pray that my kids will feel that same reassurance. Lord, fill them with your Spirit so they can walk forward in full confidence, knowing you have overcome this world.

The LORD your God is with you,
the Mighty Warrior who saves.
He will take great delight in you;
in his love he will no longer rebuke you,
but will rejoice over you with singing. (Zeph. 3:17)

My God, you are our mighty warrior. I pray that you fill my daughter with the comfort, peace, and delight that comes with knowing you are battling for her every need, every day. Give her great comfort and delight in you.

Humble yourselves, therefore, under God's mighty hand, that he may lift you up in due time. Cast all your anxiety on him because he cares for you. (1 Pet. 5:6–7)

Father God, I know that this world has troubles. Give my child the courage to cast her troubles on you so you can lift her up with your powerful love and mercy.

––––––––––

Do not be anxious about anything, but in every situation, by prayer and petition, with thanksgiving, present your requests to God. And the peace of God, which transcends all understanding, will guard your hearts and your minds in Christ Jesus. (Phil. 4:6–7)

Lord, even on difficult days, help my child through prayer and petition to give his troubles, wants, needs, hopes, dreams, and emotions to you. Fill him with your peace. Guard his mind, heart, and hopes with your perfect love.

––––––––––

• • • • •

Prayers for Myself

So do not fear, for I am with you;
    do not be dismayed, for I am your God.
I will strengthen you and help you;
    I will uphold you with my righteous right hand.
        (Isa. 41:10)

God, I know that with your strength, I can overcome any struggle. One of my biggest struggles as a mom is giving my children's pain, conflicts, and emotions over to you. I want so badly to protect them, to control their lives. But I know that you have what's best for them. Thank you for your righteousness and for holding me up so I can walk forward in your strength and trust you with my kids' struggles.

As for God, his way is perfect:
    The LORD's word is flawless;
    he shields all who take refuge in him.
For who is God besides the LORD?
    And who is the Rock except our God?
It is God who arms me with strength
    and keeps my way secure.
He makes my feet like the feet of a deer;
    he causes me to stand on the heights.
He trains my hands for battle;
    my arms can bend a bow of bronze.
You make your saving help my shield,
    and your right hand sustains me;
    your help has made me great.
You provide a broad path for my feet,
    so that my ankles do not give way. (Ps. 18:30–36)

Father God, your ways are perfect and flawless. When I'm struggling, I know you are God. You are my rock. You have secured me with strength and fought my battles for me, you have shielded me from this world, and you have saved me by your grace. You are my protector, my provider, my everything.

I will deliver you, and you will honor me. (Ps. 50:15)

Almighty God, you have promised again and again that you will deliver your people. I thank you for delivering me. Give me a supernatural vision so I can see you even on my most difficult days and turn to you even in the midst of my strongest emotions. I pray I will honor you with my faith.

6

when my child is troubled

"A mother is only as happy as her most miserable child."

Since I'm the mom and stepmom of four kids, this quote would seem to guarantee that I am pretty miserable about 90 percent of the time. One of the hardest things we go through on planet earth is watching our kids suffer. Whether it's a bad grade, a bad breakup, or the fallout from bad decisions, watching our kids suffer is one of the most painful things we as parents do.

All of Roger's and my kids have been college bound at some point, but since none of them really had a firm grasp on what they wanted to do with their lives, we encouraged them to get the first two years of college under their belt at our local junior college. We are fortunate to have a nationally ranked top twenty junior college in our community (in fact, a lot of people think it's better than many state schools in our area), so it seemed like a great plan for the kids to start there.

And it worked for everyone—except for Kimberly.

Kimberly wanted the whole "college experience"—dorm room, cafeteria food, living on campus, and staying up until four a.m. pranking the guys' dorm. She had the grades to make it into our local state university, so for her freshman year, she went.

But Kimber's dream was nothing like the reality. She hated living in the dorms. A direct quote from her: "You never know how many people have such terrible taste in music until you live in a dorm." While she loved her roommate, she had a hard time putting up with all the chaos and noise that comes with living in a dorm. Plus it was really, really expensive.

So the next year, she moved into an apartment with several other roommates. The commuting back and forth to campus, a very tumultuous relationship with her boyfriend, and a part-time job were just too much for her. Her grades crumbled, and she was not allowed to return for the following year.

Kim was devastated, ashamed, and embarrassed. She was afraid of having to confess to her dad (who was paying much of Kimberly's expenses while she was at school) about her situation. She didn't want to tell her friends that she was taking the backwards route: straight from a state school to a junior college.

Because Kimberly was devastated, I was too. Oh, I knew this wasn't the end of the world. I'm finding out that more and more kids have huge troubles their first year or two at a four-year college. I knew that she could gather herself up, finish her two-year degree at the junior college, and move forward.

But I was still devastated because Kimberly was. It's so hard to see your child in pain, and as a mom all I wanted to do was make it all better.

When My Child Is Troubled, I Feel Protective

When Kimberly's college career crumbled, my gut reaction was to call up the school. Or maybe to call up her boyfriend. I wanted to protect Kimberly from all the pain and hurt and embarrassment.

But we all know as parents that there is a line we shouldn't cross when it comes to protecting our child.

That line is invisible when our child is born. We will protect them from anything and everything—from big dangers to making sure the snap on their onesie isn't hitting them in the wrong place.

But as our children get older, that line gets a bit darker. We allow our baby to go through discomfort so she learns to sleep through the night. We allow our toddler to get upset when he has to share his prized train with a visiting friend. When our fourth grader forgets to put his homework in his backpack, we let him take the zero instead of running the page out to school.

I need to pause on that last one. I was a homework-running mom. I actually did run my son's homework out to his school a time or two (or twelve). I wanted him to get good grades because he worked on the homework, and I didn't want him to fail. It took me a long time to realize that as long as I was running his homework out to school, Justen was never feeling the pain—only I was. I was trying to protect him instead of letting him feel the kickback of his mistakes. But as researcher Brené Brown writes, "I no longer see [parental] rescuing and intervening as unhelpful, I now think about it as dangerous."[3]

When our kids reach adulthood, that line becomes Sharpie dark. I can go ahead and tell you that I've learned from experience (multiple times) that there is very (very) little we should be doing to protect our adult children. The catch is that if you've spent your life running your child's homework to school, this can be an incredibly hard transition to make.

When My Child Is Troubled, I Feel Protective, but God Is My Refuge

> My salvation and my honor depend on God;
> he is my mighty rock, my refuge.

> Trust in him at all times, you people;
> pour out your hearts to him,
> for God is our refuge. (Ps. 62:7–8)

When it comes to protecting my kids, especially as they've gotten older, I realize that the best thing I can do is put them in the safest place they could possibly be: at the feet of Jesus.

Sounds simple, doesn't it? Actually, it's something I have to do over and over again, because the reality is no matter how many times I put them squarely at the feet of Jesus, I have to use all my power—and a lot of prayer—to keep from snatching them back up again.

As parents, we would never keep our babies from learning to walk just because we are scared they could fall down. (I'm convinced their falling down is the reason God made toddlers built low to the ground.) It's not that we aren't sad when they fall and cry, but we encourage them to get back up and try again, because we know there is no other way. We know that we can't learn to walk for them and that there is no way we can hope they just "get it" as they get older. They have to walk, and to do so they have to stumble, they have to fall down, and they have to get up again.

I'm sure every mom who is reading this feels the same as I do about walking. But when it comes to our children's disappointments and troubles in life, we have a lot harder time letting them stumble and letting them fall down. Oh, we know it's going to happen, but some of us are the emotional equivalent of a mom who is running in front of her toddler with a pile of pillows, saying, "You may fall down, but you will never experience any pain as long as I'm around!"

It's a painful time in any child's life when they have to stop being rescued by their parents. That doesn't mean their parents can't help them out. That doesn't mean there is no love, no grace, no mercy. But they stop looking to their parents to take care of needs they should be taking care of themselves.

Ultimately, we want to rely on God as our protector and to be a model for our kids so they'll sit under his protection. When we let go of them, are we sure they're going to rely on God? No. But if we never let go, they will never have the need to.

This is the hard-core parenting work. The stuff where we have to allow our kids to not always like us. Where we have to say, "I'm sorry that life is so hard. I love you and I'm praying for you, but I'm not running your homework out to you (or paying your parking ticket, or . . .)."

Compared to God, we make lousy protectors for our kids, but Psalm 91:1–16 tells us all about the kind of shelter that God can be for us and for our children:

> Whoever dwells in the shelter of the Most High
> will rest in the shadow of the Almighty.
> I will say of the LORD, "He is my refuge and my fortress,
> my God, in whom I trust."
> Surely he will save you
> from the fowler's snare
> and from the deadly pestilence.
> He will cover you with his feathers,
> and under his wings you will find refuge;
> his faithfulness will be your shield and rampart.
> You will not fear the terror of night,
> nor the arrow that flies by day,
> nor the pestilence that stalks in the darkness,
> nor the plague that destroys at midday.
> A thousand may fall at your side,
> ten thousand at your right hand,
> but it will not come near you.
> You will only observe with your eyes
> and see the punishment of the wicked.
> If you say, "The LORD is my refuge,"
> and you make the Most High your dwelling,
> no harm will overtake you,
> no disaster will come near your tent.
> For he will command his angels concerning you
> to guard you in all your ways;

they will lift you up in their hands,
> so that you will not strike your foot against a stone.

You will tread on the lion and the cobra;
> you will trample the great lion and the serpent.

"Because he loves me," says the LORD, "I will rescue him;
> I will protect him, for he acknowledges my name.

He will call on me, and I will answer him;
> I will be with him in trouble,
> I will deliver him and honor him.

With long life I will satisfy him
> and show him my salvation."

A Story from the Trenches

"But, Mom, this means I can't go! It's impossible!" Annemarie wails, tears coursing down her cheeks.

Five minutes ago, she was all smiles as we sat at the kitchen table to crunch numbers for the school-sponsored ten-day trip to Italy. As we calculated the number of hours she'd have to work to earn enough money to pay for the trip, though, her face fell, her eyes reddened, and she reached for the Kleenex.

Pain and disappointment can be effective teachers, I remind myself. *Don't cave. No matter how badly you want to bail her out—for your sake as well as hers—don't rescue her. These are natural consequences; this kind of pain and disappointment is the okay kind.*

"Chickie," I say, trying to keep my voice steady and upbeat, "it is possible for you to earn the money. You'll just have to commit to working eight hours a day for all eight weeks of your summer break."

"But I don't want to!" she sobs back, throwing up her hands in despair. "I've been looking forward to having this summer off! It's been such a crazy school year; I deserve a break. I've worked so hard. I want time for myself!"

How I hated seeing her tears!

I start to rationalize: *She's right; it has been a rough school year. I could offer to go halfway on the trip with her. That way she'd only*

82

have to work half as much. Surely that would make her feel better. I don't want to see her hopes crushed. The Italy trip is such a great opportunity for her. . . .

Pain and disappointment can be effective teachers.

What vital lessons will I deprive her of learning if I step in to ease the current pain and disappointment? This is a great opportunity to learn how badly she actually wants the trip or if she's just been enjoying the fantasy.

Ten years ago, when I first heard a parenting expert declare, "Pain and disappointment can be effective teachers," my first reaction was deep rebellion: *No! I've spent my entire parenting life trying to protect my kids from pain and disappointment!* My own childhood included a number of instances of totally inappropriate pain and disappointment—emotional abandonment, verbal battering, physical neglect, and sexual violation—that caused me to define all pain and disappointment as harmful.

I realized that in my zeal to protect my children from the inappropriate kinds of pain and disappointment I'd experienced as a child, I had aimed to protect them from all pain and disappointment. As a result, I was raising kids who were accustomed to being rescued even from the normal process of natural consequences. Learning to tell myself this kind of pain and disappointment is the okay kind has been a difficult but vital part of my growth as a parent.

As I've learned to trust the process, Psalm 62:8 has taken on new meaning: "Trust in him at all times, you people; pour out your hearts to him, for God is our refuge."

I steel myself and quietly state, "Honey, it looks like you've got two very different choices in front of you—a forced alternative. You can either work all summer and go on the Italy trip in October, or you can take the summer off and not go on the trip. I don't know which choice is right for you; only you can decide that. I'll support you either way."

"But . . . but . . ." she cries, her volume notching up to a whole new level, "it's not fair! You said I could go! I've told everyone I'm going! It's not fair!"

I wince. The you're-letting-me-down and it's-not-fair defenses, both at once. I want out of this conversation. It's more intense than I want to deal with. What's the fastest way out? If we call Nana and Papa, they'd probably be willing to help. . . .

Pain and disappointment can be effective teachers.

What will she learn if a bit of dramatics is all it takes to "earn" a trip to Italy? What are you modeling for her if you cop out so quickly? Don't rescue her. This kind of pain and disappointment is the okay kind.

I look my daughter squarely in the eye and say, as kindly but as firmly as possible, "Unfair? It would be unfair if we'd misled you. But when we said you could go, we also said as long as you earn the money for the trip. The numbers you've just calculated aren't unfair, just really, really, really disappointing."

Nodding dumbly, Annemarie buries her face in her arms. Still fighting the let-me-make-it-all-better urge, I lean over to hug her. She stiffens—still mad—then relaxes, glad for comfort.

Trust in God at all times, daughters. Together we are learning that some kinds of pain and disappointment are effective teachers. Pour out your hearts to him, for he is our refuge. We are learning to trust and find refuge in God.

Together.

Cheri Gregory

Practical Steps

I'm willing to bet that 99.876 percent of the moms reading this have been tempted to bail their kids out at one time or a billion others. It's a natural part of motherhood, and it's something we all want to do. But when you rescue your kids, it's like taking pain meds after you've broken your arm. You feel better for a while, but not only are you not fixing the problem, you're probably making it worse. There are some big problems with that particular brand of parenting. I urge you to think about the long-term effects of being a bailout mom. Here's why:

1. **Understand that moms make lousy shelters.** When it comes to shelters, we are like cardboard refrigerator boxes. Yes, we can provide some safety. Yes, we can make a good short-term hiding place. But we're pretty flimsy and totally unresistant to the weather when storms come. We need to keep pointing our kids to our strong tower, the only true shelter that any of us ever has. Yep—that means leaving them out in the cold sometimes so they will seek a more permanent Shelter.

2. **Accept that we are not always going to be around.** I'm not trying to be morbid here, but the whole goal is for our kids to be able to go out into the world and, with a loving God, make it on their own. We want their bottom line to be Jesus, not our bank accounts, spare rooms, and fridges. Hopefully your kid will be out on their own at some point.

   I was talking to my friend Carrie recently, and she told me that when she attended her son's college orientation last week, she had to take a full eight-hour class on time management. The professor who taught it said that most college students have trouble managing their time, so the college was teaching the parents how to have time management skills so maybe they could help their kids. I don't know about you, but I see all sorts of things wrong with that idea. We want our kids to be self-sufficient. And a good first step in that direction is to stop bailing them out.

3. **Know that the easy way out isn't best.** It's tempting to take the easy way out. Why? Because it's easy. And you'd better believe if given the opportunity, your kid is going to choose easy over difficult or troubling or stressful. But easy doesn't mean better. In fact, chances are that the hard way is going to help grow your child (and you). Sometimes the teacher is right—your child was disruptive in class and needs to have

privileges taken away. Sometimes you need to be the mean mom. If this is a struggle for you, band together with other parents who can hold you accountable. Our goal is character, not comfort.

4. **Remind yourself that God's mercy is sufficient.** I'm all for being merciful. Trust me, God gave me (and most moms) the gift of mercy in spades, and I'm all for the occasional get-out-of-chores-free card. But I also constantly remind myself and my children that God's mercy is all we need. When I try to throw my mixed-up, unfounded mercy on top of God's merciful plan, I tend to muddy the waters.

●　●　●　●　●

Prayers for My Child

God is our refuge and strength,
an ever-present help in trouble. (Ps. 46:1)

Father God, you are the refuge and strength my child needs. I sometimes forget that and get caught up in how I can help him, how I can make his life easier. But the truth is he doesn't need me to be his refuge. He needs you.

No temptation has overtaken you except what is common to mankind. And God is faithful; he will not let you be tempted beyond what you can bear. But when you are tempted, he will also provide a way out so that you can endure it. (1 Cor. 10:13)

Father God, I know there is no temptation in this world that is beyond your control. Even as my kids struggle through times of trouble, help them to be comforted by the fact that you always provide a way for your children. Give them the wisdom to lean on you when they don't have the strength to carry on.

———————————

The LORD reigns forever;
  he has established his throne for judgment.
He rules the world in righteousness
  and judges the peoples with equity.
The LORD is a refuge for the oppressed,
  a stronghold in times of trouble.
Those who know your name trust in you,
    for you, LORD, have never forsaken those who seek
    you. (Ps. 9:7–10)

Reigning God, as troubling as our world can be, I know that you rule it in righteousness. Be a stronghold for my daughter as she faces times of trouble. Be her refuge, her shelter, her peace. Lord, you have never forsaken those who seek you, and I pray that my daughter will seek you earnestly so she can feel your blessing fully.

———————————

At my first defense, no one came to my support, but everyone deserted me. May it not be held against them. But the Lord stood at my side and gave me strength, so that through me the message might be fully proclaimed and all the Gentiles might hear it. And I was delivered from the lion's mouth. The Lord will rescue me from every evil attack and will bring me safely to his heavenly kingdom. To him be glory for ever and ever. (2 Tim. 4:16–18)

Father God, sometimes the trouble of this world seems insurmountable. It seems as if we simply can't endure. My baby, my precious child, is feeling that way now. Lord, come beside her. Help her to see that you are her deliverer. Show her that you will rescue her from any evil in this world and bring her safely into your fold. I love that I can trust you fully to be her defender, her protector, and her tower of strength and hope.

---

* * * * *

Prayers for Myself

But as for me, it is good to be near God.
I have made the Sovereign LORD my refuge;
I will tell of all your deeds. (Ps. 73:28)

Sovereign Lord, you are so good! You have been a refuge for me in times of trouble, a beacon of hope in times of despair. I want to share the delight I have in you with my kids. I rejoice in you, and I want every word I say and everything I do to be a reflection of your good works so my children too will learn to lean on you as their source of strength.

This I declare about the LORD:
He alone is my refuge, my place of safety;
he is my God, and I trust him. (Ps. 91:2 NLT)

Lord God, you are my only place of safety. I trust you to carry my burdens fully, and I pray that you do the same for my kids. Please forgive me when my pride takes over and I try to solve problems on my own. Remind me that I can trust you and that I do not need to stand on my own power.

The LORD is my strength and my defense;
    he has become my salvation.
He is my God, and I will praise him,
    my father's God, and I will exalt him. (Exod. 15:2)

You are my strength, O God. You have saved me from my own sin, and you have defended me when I deserved no defense. I exalt you, O Lord, because you are worthy to be praised.

O God, listen to my cry!
    Hear my prayer!
From the ends of the earth,
    I cry to you for help
    when my heart is overwhelmed.
Lead me to the towering rock of safety,
    for you are my safe refuge,
    a fortress where my enemies cannot reach me. (Ps.
        61:1–3 NLT)

My Lord, my God, hear my prayers! My heart is overwhelmed when my kids are troubled. I ache for them. I want to jump to their defense, to fight their battles, to lay out a smooth and easy path. But I know that isn't right because I am not their refuge—you are. You are my rock of safety and my fortress of strength. No trouble can reach me when I rest in you.

Then I pray to you, O LORD.
    I say, "You are my place of refuge.
    You are all I really want in life." (Ps. 142:5 NLT)

O Lord, you are my place of refuge. You are all I need in life. Each time trouble comes my way, help me immediately turn to you in praise and trust you fully to deal with the trouble in the way that you in your infinite wisdom know best. I believe if I can trust you to carry me, I can survive anything.

7

when my child is sick or injured

I was sitting in the lobby of a great doctor's office. (How did I know it was a great office? The magazine selection was totally up-to-date and varied. They even had that week's *People* and *Entertainment Weekly*. There must have been about fifty different issues to choose from.) I was waiting for my daughter to emerge from the procedures room with four fewer wisdom teeth.

I don't consider myself an anxious mom when it comes to the whole doctor thing. After all, these were just wisdom teeth—many people have them removed at one point or another, right? So I had sent Kimberly into the back room filled up on prayer and with a cheerful, "See you in a little bit! Love you!" and planned to dive into the latest issue of *Cooking Light*.

As I causally flipped through the light chicken piccata recipes, my mind kept being drawn back to Kimberly. And that's when I started to worry.

I worried because I knew how difficult my wisdom tooth extraction was (impacted teeth followed by painful dry sockets after the surgery), and I knew that Kimber has an abnormally high sensitivity to pain. (Her regular dentist usually needs to give her about three shots to get her numb.) I worried because of all the medications she was taking. I worried because things could go wrong. But mostly I worried because I had no control over the situation. And I worried because that's what moms do. Worry.

Don't all of us moms do that? We remember the pain that we experience, whether it's the removal of a wisdom tooth or the pain of a broken heart, and immediately take on our kid's pain.

Strangers had my baby in that back room, and they were cutting her open. Would they take care of her? Would they work quickly if something went wrong? I wanted to run back there and make sure everything was going the way it was supposed to. I confess, I was losing my mind. All because of worry.

Seeing as how I'm a writer and not an oral surgeon, I wasn't up on my dental procedures, but there was something deep inside of me that wanted to go back there and take things into my own hands. How often have I wanted to take that control—not only for my children's health but for every area of their lives—out of God's hands and put it into my own? Quite often, if I'm honest.

Imagine if it were more than a few impacted teeth.

As a parent, I haven't had a lot of experience with my kids truly being sick. We've had a couple of car accidents (and in each of those incidents, our kids called us and started the conversation with, "Don't freak out, I'm all right, but I've been in an accident . . .") and a couple of trips to the emergency room (because apparently that's required in order to get your parent card punched), but nothing major. But I still worry.

It's part of being a mom. Even if your child has sustained nothing more than a skinned knee, I'm guessing that you've spent plenty of time worrying about the possibility of something happening. Moms are notorious worriers, and that's why I addressed worrying right up front. But in this chapter, we're going to focus on how to pray for your kids when they truly are sick or injured, whether it's a tiny cold or a major emergency. Because (need I remind you?) prayer is your most powerful tool not only against worry but also for health and safety.

When My Child Is Sick or Injured, I Realize I'm Helpless

Please, God, please, God, please . . .

It's a desperate prayer that I think every mom has prayed at one time or another. *Please, God, keep my kids safe. Please, God, don't let them get hurt. Please, God, don't let them do anything stupid today. Please, please, please.*

Accidents happen. We all know that. For us moms, it's hard not to worry about our kids getting hurt. Trusting God with our kids' safety is one of the most difficult things we can do as moms, but it's also one of the most important. While it's natural to want to protect our children, God wants us to trust him with our precious treasures.

In this chapter, I'm going to share stories, prayers, and ideas to remind you to hand your kids' safety over to God in a way that will not only ease your worried spirit but also help you take steps toward trusting God in a more intimate way.

When My Child Is Sick or Injured, I Realize I'm Helpless, but God Is My Comforter

> Praise be to the God and Father of our Lord Jesus Christ, the Father of compassion and the God of all comfort, who comforts us in all our troubles, so that we can comfort those in any trouble with the comfort we ourselves receive from God. For just as we share abundantly in the sufferings of Christ, so also our comfort abounds through Christ. (2 Cor. 1:3–5)

I worried about my kids' safety most when my son was young. There's something about a four-year-old boy that just screams "accident waiting to happen," and I woke up every day with this heavy burden of fear in my heart that Justen was going to break something or cut something or bruise something. I confess, my fear and worry were borderline untrusting at times.

I remember a day at the park as he swung kamikaze from the monkey bars. I hovered under him, angling my body with his every move so that if he did take the plunge, I could cushion his fall with my body. Yes. I did that. And after the fourth time I screamed, "Be careful!" I realized that all I was doing was helicoptering my way into craziness by not trusting God to be my son's healer. And while I didn't quit cold turkey on my worrying and fretting, I did make my way away from those dangerous monkey bars and onto a shaded park bench where I could watch Justen's antics from a distance and pray.

It's a terrible thing for moms to realize that sometimes, when it comes to protecting our kids, we are helpless.

My prayer started like it always did: "Please, God, please . . ." But then I allowed him to work in my heart. To move my prayer to "I trust you, Lord" and "You love him more than I do, Lord," then to "Lord, help me to be the mom he needs to keep him safe physically, emotionally, and spiritually" to "God, you are his healer. There is nothing you can't do!" God removed the worry from my heart and replaced it with trust. He removed the pleading from my words and replaced it with hope.

But Justen was just my practice child. I should have known that God was preparing me for a bigger challenge. That challenge was named Kimberly.

On her first birthday, Kimber decided to celebrate with a leap from her crib and a trip to the emergency room. Her head was bleeding, and the pain, guilt, and terror of wondering what was going to happen flooded over me. It was only when another mom in the room next to us came over and—without ever speaking directly to me—started praying over us that my focus was able to shift.

Yes, Kimber was in my arms, but that wasn't the safest place for her. At the feet of Jesus, covered in prayer by the words of a stranger, was where she (and I) needed to be.

The Bible is full of examples where Jesus healed. But it's also full of places where healing came later—in heaven, where God's glorious plan was truly revealed. Think about Elizabeth, John the Baptist's mom. Read Luke 1:5–25 and you'll see the incredible gift that John was in her life. He was a miracle baby—everything she had prayed for and hoped for her entire life. And he was wonderful. But his miraculous birth sharply contrasted with the horrendous death he faced thirty years later.

There is always a "what if" here: What if God doesn't heal? What if he chooses not to work a miracle? I know it's hard to even think about—it is for me—but God did not promise a perfectly healthy life to those who love him. He gives us obvious moments of joy—those first steps, those first words, that first day of school—but there is also pain in this world. And while we want to cling hard to our kids (it's that control thing again), we also have to trust God's incredible plan. And that's what praying for our kids when they are hurt is all about. Not healing but trust, comfort, and reassurance that God is God, and he knows you and your child inside and out.

I have learned through the years that simply the best thing we can do when we're worried about our kids' safety is turn to the only one who truly can protect them and comfort us. Say it with me: "Lord, I give my kids to you."

A Story from the Trenches

Just another day. We headed to my sister's house to take a walk we've taken many times before. My parents were in town to help my sister through a husband-less week with her four babes, and we wanted to celebrate Fat Tuesday with a pancake dinner. My husband was in the Midwest for work. We were ready for Valentine's Day parties at school the next day.

As we headed toward the playground on scooters, going south on the residential sidewalk, my sweet niece rode her scooter through a cross street without stopping for adult approval. My Eve paused long enough to say, "Mommy, I bet you're proud of me for being safe." I assured her I was very proud.

One block later my Eve was a house length ahead of me on her scooter when a pickup truck heading down the street decided to hop into reverse and swing backwards into the driveway my little baby was scooting past.

In slow motion, I remember my dad saying something under his breath about the driver. I have a split-second memory of thinking he was worried about nothing. I didn't see what he saw. I didn't see what was about to happen. I never could have imagined it.

Eve even saw the truck coming, and at the last second she hopped off her scooter and ran backwards as I ran screaming down the street. The kind of scream that a neighbor cringes to hear. The scream of a terrified mother worried about losing the most precious gift she has ever been trusted to love. As I watched her tumble under the truck, my mind went white. I was clawing at my dad, screaming, "Call 911!" so loudly that I think it was nearly silent.

I climbed under the truck to find her. She was trapped beneath the running truck with the metal bar of her scooter pinning her to the sidewalk. She couldn't breathe but she could scream. They were the hardest worst saddest scariest longest shortest minutes of my life. I couldn't stop the truck. I couldn't get her out from underneath.

I couldn't protect her, but God did. He held her safely in the palm of his hand while the world tumbled around her. The accident was not a surprise to him, and he held her tight and most of all *safe*.

Once we freed the scooter from its wedged spot under the truck, I clawed my way to her and pulled her, shaking, onto my lap. I laid on my back on the pavement with her on top, too scared to look at her face to see where the blood was coming from. Not ready to know if her face would ever look the same, if her physical body was changed forever. Just holding her spirit. I found myself praying out loud, rocking on the sidewalk.

As the ambulance pulled up, there came the realization that I had two other children watching this horrible moment. It hit me hard. I saw them down the block being loved by my dad, mom, and sister, and I was immensely grateful that even if I couldn't stop their tears, they were with people who love them just like I do.

The ride to the hospital. X-rays. C-collars. MRIs. Pain management. Retelling the one story I wanted to completely forget over and over for each new professional who entered our room. How can a memory soften and have grace when you have to remind yourself every hour? Hearing that cry. Remembering the panic. My shaking hands. Her beating heart.

Today Eve is healthy and in good spirits. She has a skull fracture and three vertebrae fractures. We will know more and we will manage it.

Us? We have our Eve. My girls have their sister. We are the luckiest people in town. We have been wrapped in the love and prayers of our friends in a way I never imagined possible. We are blessed.

Mollie Burpo

Practical Steps

How can we pray for our children's safety without letting worry and fear overtake our hearts? Here are some tips:

1. **Pray and then pray some more.** Are you starting to see a pattern? Praying is my first tip in many chapters because praying for our kids and (just as importantly) for ourselves is the most important thing we can do. As a mom, you can't keep your kids safe. There is no prayer that is going to guarantee healing. But you can guarantee comfort, peace, and a God who knows what's best. It is not a show of unfaithfulness to be concerned. You also can't remove the worry from your heart. But God can be your comfort in any of these circumstances. And only through earnest and intimate prayer can he truly move in you.

2. **Understand that this is hard stuff. Also understand that people don't know what to say when your child is hurting.** People are going to try to be comforting. That comes from a good place for the most part. But people don't know what to say. They talk about their relative who was miraculously healed or their dog that had the same kind of injury. Ugh. I've said some of those kinds of things because I didn't know what to say.

3. **Ask for prayer. And spaghetti.** At the hardest times in life, when people offer to make meals or clean your bathroom, let them. You need support, and people want to help. It helps you and it helps them.

4. **Give them the prayers below, or give them verses that are meaningful to you.** People who don't know what to say want to help. Let them help whenever possible. They want something tangible to do, so ask them for prayer. When you are too worn out to pray, have others pray for you. Gather your troops—in person, at church, or on Facebook—and let people know what is going on. This is hard and you need encouragement.

• • • • •

Prayers for My Child

In peace I will lie down and sleep,
for you alone, LORD,
make me dwell in safety. (Ps. 4:8)

Prince of Peace, Mighty God, thank you for protecting me and my kids. Thank you for the peace, the hope, and the rest that come from knowing you are God. I pray that my child will know you and your character more and more deeply each day.

If you say, "The LORD is my refuge,"
    and you make the Most High your dwelling,
no harm will overtake you,
    no disaster will come near your tent.
For he will command his angels concerning you
    to guard you in all your ways;
they will lift you up in their hands,
    so that you will not strike your foot against a stone.
You will tread on the lion and the cobra;
    you will trample the great lion and the serpent. (Ps.
        91:9–13)

Father God, you never guarantee my kids' physical safety in the Bible, but you do promise spiritual safety for anyone who abides in you. And so, Lord God, I turn my heart and my soul over to you every day. Guard it with your perfect strength. Likewise, light a fire in my kids to turn their spiritual safety over to you so they can do not what's safe or easy in this life but what's right for the next. Lord, I trust you to hold my precious children in your all-powerful hand.

Therefore if you have any encouragement from being united with Christ, if any comfort from his love, if any common sharing in the Spirit, if any tenderness and compassion, then make my joy complete by being like-minded, having the same love, being one in spirit and of one mind. Do nothing out of selfish ambition or vain conceit. Rather, in humility value others above yourselves, not looking to your own interests but each of you to the interests of the others. (Phil. 2:1–4)

O God, I take comfort in your love. I am encouraged by your promises. I pray that my kids will be filled with you so they too can feel the joy that comes from fully trusting you. Help me not to make decisions out of selfishness—out of a desire to control or protect my kids or out of a spirit of worry—but instead out of a desire to honor you.

Paul, a servant of God and an apostle of Jesus Christ to further the faith of God's elect and their knowledge of the truth that leads to godliness—in the hope of eternal life, which God, who does not lie, promised before the beginning of time, and which now at his appointed season he has brought to light through the preaching entrusted to me by the command of God our Savior. (Titus 1:1–3)

Lord, you make it clear that knowledge and truth lead to godliness, and godliness leads to eternal life. You don't promise an easy life on earth, but you do promise eternity with you. I want that for my kids more than anything. I pray that in this season of their lives, you will shed your light on them. Yes, Lord, if it's your will, keep them safe and healthy, but even more importantly, grow in their hearts a spiritual health that leads to a desire for you.

● ● ● ● ●

Prayers for Myself

Have I not commanded you? Be strong and courageous. Do not be afraid; do not be discouraged, for the Lord your God will be with you wherever you go. (Josh. 1:9)

*Omniscient God, I will not walk in fear. You have com-
manded us to be strong and courageous, so I will be.
Take away my fear so I can live in full hope and peace
in you. I am not afraid! You have promised that you
will be with me and with my kids wherever we go. You
have a plan. You have things under control. With that
promise I can rest peacefully, knowing you are God.*

One night the LORD spoke to Paul in a vision: "Do not
be afraid; keep on speaking, do not be silent. For I am
with you, and no one is going to attack and harm you,
because I have many people in this city." So Paul stayed
in Corinth for a year and a half, teaching them the word
of God. (Acts 18:9–11)

*You are our great protector. I pray that I would have
the courage to love deeply, to speak honestly, to trust
wholly, and to hope fully when it comes to my children.
I know our world is a scary place, but you have overcome our world! I pray that you give me the confidence
to trust you when it comes to my kids' health so I can
love them like you do.*

Then Jesus came to them and said, "All authority in heaven
and on earth has been given to me. Therefore go and make
disciples of all nations, baptizing them in the name of the
Father and of the Son and of the Holy Spirit, and teaching them to obey everything I have commanded you. And
surely I am with you always, to the very end of the age."
(Matt. 28:18–20)

*Lord Jesus, you have all authority in the world. You
are in charge of everything. Everything! Which means
that all things—great and small—are under your*

all-knowing, all-loving, and all-powerful hand. Thank you! Lord, give me the courage and peace to make disciples of my kids without worrying about the things of this world. Help me to teach them about you so they can begin to understand your glory and the hope they have in you.

8

when my child makes poor choices

There are two kinds of poor choices. The first kind, your run-of-the-mill "I forgot to brush my teeth before school today" and "I didn't study very hard for my math test" are rather benign. You dig out the Brush-Ups you have stashed in the minivan, explain that poor grades means less time on the computer, and go on with your day. If your kid is just making the kind of poor choice that can be amended by picking up a pack of gum on the way to school, then you've hit the parenting jackpot. Chalk it up to good parenting, skip this chapter, and go make yourself a congratulatory latte. Kidding. You should really brace yourself for what's sure to come.

Because there's another kind of poor choice. The kind of poor choice that screams, "I'm dead set on doing anything and everything I can to give my poor mama a heart attack." And (don't shoot the messenger) I'm willing to go out on a limb and say that every kid in the world will make this type of poor choice at least once or twenty-seven times in his juvenile career.

I'm not trying to make light of this—when your kid starts making poor choices, it's serious—but I do want to reassure you that like your Tae Bo phase and that weird curly thing you used to do with your hair, this too most likely shall pass. And in the meantime, I want to help you pray your kid through it.

When My Child Makes Poor Choices, I Feel Powerless

I have a very well-behaved puggle name Jake. Jake and rules get along very well. In fact, Jake will pretty much do whatever I say as long as there is minimal petting or a treat involved. Jake loves me enough to follow the rules because he wants to make me happy.

Our new kitten, Ash, however, is just the opposite. She couldn't care less about making me happy. And if she wants to climb to the top of my brand-new Pottery Barn curtains just to see how many claw marks she can etch into them, then you can bet she's going to do it proudly, loudly, and right in front of me with a nefarious kitty smirk on her face. And it doesn't matter if I bribe her with salmon-drizzled catnip; if she wants to do something, you better believe that nothing as trivial as my displeasure is going to keep her from committing her dastardly deed.

My point? Kids are like kittens and not like puggles. They may be all cute and slobbery when they're little, but by the time they're eighteen months old, there is nothing you can do as a mom that will force them to make good choices. You can try—a good dose of logical consequences and chocolate-covered bribery can work wonders with kids—but unless they are intrinsically motivated to make the right choice, you're probably out of luck.

If you're anything like me, the inability to guarantee your kids make good choices probably makes you feel powerless. That wouldn't sit well with me if I didn't have God to lean on, because—you guessed it—I may not be in control, but God is.

I felt exactly like this—powerless to make good choices for my children—when my stepdaughter Amanda dropped the bomb into conversation ever so subtly. "Yeah, Shaun and I are looking for an apartment in Palo Alto."

Um . . . what?

Please tell me this is a girl named Shaun—like Shauna . . .

Nope. It was her boyfriend. Amanda was moving in with her boyfriend.

And our hearts just hurt.

We liked Shaun. Amanda had been engaged to another young man before Shaun, and let's just say Roger and I spent a lot of time praying that this particular boy would just go away. And he did. I'll be honest—we felt like the parents of the year. We prayed the wrong guy out.

Shaun was a great fit for Amanda. One of the first things they did when they started dating was to find a local church. Huzzah! We liked Shaun, we prayed for their relationship, and we were excited to see what God had in store.

After a couple of years of dating, living together is what Amanda and Shaun had in store.

I hate to admit it, but my first reaction was, *Ugh. Everyone is going to think we're horrible parents.* (Perhaps a bit self-centered, Kathi?) It's embarrassing to think that I was concerned about our reputation before how this poor choice was going to affect Amanda and Shaun, but it's the truth. I'm sure I'm not the only one who has thought first, *What will the other moms at school, my parents, my friends at work, etc., think?*

Another reason it was so hard was that we had no control over the situation—here were two adults making big decisions, and while Amanda loves us and respects us in many areas, she let us know up front that we wouldn't change her mind.

Amanda and Shaun know exactly how we feel about them living together. But they also know exactly how we feel about them.

Our discussions with them, while not perfect, have gone something like this: "We hate that you are living together, but we love you. The reason that we hate it is because it's less than God's loving plan for your life. We know that us talking to you about this is probably not going to change your minds, but because we love you and you love us, we get to speak into your lives on this situation." So we keep talking and listening and loving them and praying for them.

But to be honest, this hasn't lessened the embarrassment of having to explain the "situation" to others. Even though we get to say what we want to say and we talk openly about it, Shaun and Amanda living together makes us feel like we've failed as parents.

The lack of control over kids (adult and younger) is one of the hardest things I've ever experienced as a parent. Oh, it would just be so much easier if my kids were living their lives to please me!

When My Child Makes Poor Choices, I Feel Powerless, but God Is My Rock

> Truly my soul finds rest in God;
> my salvation comes from him.
> Truly he is my rock and my salvation;
> he is my fortress, I will never be shaken. (Ps. 62:1–2)

It's easy to say that God is my rock, but it's much harder to live that out day to day. I often gauge how *I'm* doing in life by how my kids are doing in life. It's easy to construct our lives on those of our children. To let them determine our peace of mind, our worthiness as people. It's easy to let our kids be the gauge of how much God loves us and how obedient we've been. It makes sense, right? If I do everything right, if I live by God's promises and proverbs, my kids will turn out right.

That thinking gets us into trouble.

Yes, God gives us his principles and promises for a reason. I wake up every day wanting to live closer to his loving plan for my life. But if I look at my kids as a direct result of the choices I've made, I'm going to have an incomplete picture of who God is and what he is doing in my life—and in theirs.

When we build our lives on anything other than the Rock who is Jesus Christ, we are going to crumble, just like the homes built on sand that Jesus talks about in Matthew 7:24–27. It takes so much more intention, so much more prayer, to build our house on the Rock. But if we do, then when our child decides to cheat on a test, or tries drugs, or gets pregnant, our whole world does not come crashing down. Yes, it's painful; yes, it's going to take some time to recover. But we haven't put our trust in our child's choices. We've put our trust in the Rock.

How do you know that you've placed your trust in your child's choices? Here are some signs:

1. When people ask you how you're doing, you immediately give them a list of your child's accomplishments or misdeeds.
2. Your mood is tied into your child's mood. If they're having a good day, you're having a good day. If they're miserable, so are you.
3. There are days where you give in to your child because it's easier than disappointing them.
4. When your child receives a certain grade, you feel like it's a direct result (good or bad) of your parenting.

You can't force your kid to make good choices. And if you're being honest, God can't either. He is pretty firm with that whole free will thing. But God can work miracles in your kids' lives so they'll want to make good choices.

God gave your kids freedom to make their own choices—not because he wanted them to spend next Saturday night making a bonfire out of your couch cushions but because he wanted them to have the ability to follow him in an authentic and real way. At times, that means having the freedom to make the choices that will teach them the most about him.

The last thing I want to do is advocate for your kids' poor choices, but I do want to encourage you that God can and will work with your kids—poor choices and all. God has not and will not give up on your kids. Instead of getting angry or depressed or hopeless, you can choose to be a strong advocate, a prayer warrior, an encourager, a hoper. Because regardless of what your kids are doing now, I can assure you that God is doing much, much more.

Something I've needed to remember is that throughout all my own bad choices as a child, God never left me. He never abandoned me. I didn't live with my boyfriend, but that didn't stop me from getting pregnant before I was married. At the time I thought (and I'm guessing my mom thought) that my life was over. Were there consequences for my poor choices? Absolutely. Was God able to restore the circumstances of my life? Absolutely!

God has shown again and again that he is willing to stick by each of us through thick and thin, good and bad. Look at Bathsheba and David (2 Samuel 11). They sinned greatly—David actually went so far as to have a man killed just so he could cover up his own adultery. And they did face consequences for their actions—I'm sure that there were some sleepless nights when both Bathsheba and David felt like their lives were ruined. But God picked up the pieces. He stood by them and restored them and, in the end, used them greatly for his kingdom. And he can and will do the same for your kids.

A Story from the Trenches

I have a theory about Walmart. I believe that they pipe in some sort of air containing a chemical that causes adults to lose all sense of pride and what is socially acceptable, and causes small children to become screaming, wriggling sacks of goo. It's only a theory at this point, but the website PeopleOfWalmart.com coupled with my own experiences lends credence to it.

Case in point: March 31, 2006.

We walked into the store. I put Princess, my six-year-old daughter, in the back of a shopping cart and Buddy, my almost-three-year-old son, in the front. I picked up some necessities like toilet paper and cat food. And then, because the kids had behaved, we stopped in the school supply section for a prize of watercolors. I handed each of them their tray, and they gazed upon the colors with wonder. Then Buddy began to bang his on the front of the cart.

I told him not to bang the paints.

Bang, bang, bang.

Obviously he hadn't heard me or I just hadn't given a good enough explanation. (I didn't want to be the type of mom who says, "Because I said so!") So I told him that if he slammed the paints on the cart, he might break them, and then he wouldn't be able to use them.

Bang, bang, bang.

Okay, he heard me tell him to stop and then he heard me tell him why. Now it was just about obedience. I told him that if he slammed the paints on the cart one more time, I'd take them away from him and put them in the back with Princess.

Bang, bang, bang.

I calmly took the paints from him and put them in the back of the cart with his sister. Buddy began the cart twist move—trying to twist around in the seat and maneuver out of the seatbelt that is more ornamental than functional. All the while, he was wailing.

I told Buddy that if he continued to twist around and yell, I would put the paints back on the shelf and he wouldn't get them.

Twist, yell, twist, scream.

Back went the paints.

The horror. The horror.

Now Buddy was screaming at the top of his lungs and twisting around with such vehemence that it was getting dangerous. I took him out of the cart and put him on the floor. He immediately threw himself on my feet, sobbing and wailing. Because I had been reading a book on behavior, I immediately deduced that at this point his fit was about attention and, in order to quell the storm, I must ignore it because even negative attention is attention. I slowly walked three steps to my right and browsed the Scotch tape (wondering if anyone would notice if I used it over his mouth). He crawled on hands and knees and once again flung himself on my feet. I calmly stepped away and moved back toward the cart, wondering if there was any way on God's green earth that the store was populated entirely by deaf individuals.

Buddy crawled back to me and collapsed once again. Silently cursing the stupid parenting book that I had wasted so much time on, I decided that we just needed to get the heck outta Dodge. I scooped Buddy up with one arm and pushed the cart with the other, heading for the checkout. Because we really did need that toilet paper.

I couldn't risk putting Buddy down. He was too out of control. So I kept him on my hip as I took the items out of my cart and put them on the conveyer belt. I was not paying enough attention to Buddy or his fit, so he decided that he'd get my attention again. He bit me. Yes, you read that right. He sank his teeth into my shoulder. Hard enough for me to cry out and instinctively swat his head. I gritted my teeth and told him not to do that again. He ignored me.

At this point, I had absolutely no idea what to do. I had *that* kid. That out-of-control, screaming-to-the-point-of-discoloration kid. Everyone was looking at me. Most were looking at me with sympathy as if to tell me that they had been there. However, I do remember one lady looking at me with such scorn and ridicule that I almost walked over to her, handed Buddy to her, and said, "Okay, *you* do it!" But at that point I was just ready to leave.

After a couple more of his bites, I put Buddy down on the ground. But I didn't let him go. I kept a firm grip on his little wrist because I had absolutely no idea what he would do or where he would go were he free. He promptly bit my hand. Then he whirled around, and—I am *not* kidding—he bit my butt.

That brought me to some sort of reality. I saw the complete absurdity of the whole thing and I actually relaxed just a bit. I picked up Buddy (and my shoulder got a few more teeth marks), paid for our items, took the screaming little mass outside to the car, and wrestled him into the car seat. Then his screams started to be coherent.

He had begun yelling, "Stupid! Stupid! Stupid!" I was perplexed for a moment until I realized that *stupid* was the worst word he knew. He was cussing at me.

He had calmed down a little by the time we pulled into the driveway. I got him out of the car and took him immediately to his room, where he screamed for another half hour before he fell asleep.

Of course I called my husband to tell him all that had happened. When he got home, I showed him the bruises on my shoulder (yes, I had quite a few nasty bite bruises). My husband sat Buddy down and had a pretty intense heart-to-heart. He said that I was his wife and that he was charged with taking care of me and protecting me, and he would do that no matter what. He said if Buddy ever hurt me again, he'd have to answer to my hubby. He didn't do this in a threatening way, but he did make his point.

It's been seven years since that incident. I get a lot of mileage from it! I actually enjoy telling it, and believe it or not, Buddy enjoys hearing it. He laughs and says, "I can't believe I did that!" And then sometimes he'll come and kiss my shoulder where he bit it. But we can laugh about it now because it was an isolated incident.

That was the last knock-down, drag-out fit that Buddy ever had. It could be because we gave him swift and appropriate consequences. And it could be that we continue to demand of him (and his sister) good manners and acceptable behavior.

Or it could be because we just stay out of Walmart.

Milaka Falk

Practical Steps

Aside from grounding your kids from everything that plugs in until 2023, what can you do to help them when they are making the wrong decisions? Here are a few ideas:

1. **Pray and then keep praying.** You can't make your kid do the right thing (recall Ash the kitten). You can, however, pray fervently that God will work in your kid's heart, that God will move powerfully through you, and that God will shed the light of truth on your kid.

2. **Use your tools.** God may have given your kid free will, but he gave you something more powerful: his Word. Dive into Scripture to get the insight you need to help your kid in this difficult time.

3. **Be there.** A friend's husband went to jail for criminal possession when he was nineteen. In this obviously devastating time, he said the one thing that kept him hanging on was the fact that his mother religiously wrote, called, and visited him. She never once advocated his choices, but she made sure he knew that she loved him in spite of them.

4. **Seek help for your kid.** Whether your kid needs a professional counselor or just a mentoring adult, find someone you trust who will support and stand by them.

5. **Seek help for yourself.** Mamas need some help too! Trust me, some of the most depressing, frustrating, and trying times in my life weren't when I was making poor choices (although I've made plenty) but when my kids were. When that's happening, find someone—whether it's a close friend, a pastor, or a Christian counselor—who can give you outsider advice, insight, and hope as you parent your kid through poor choices.

· · · · ·

Prayers for My Child

Many are the plans in a person's heart,
but it is the LORD's purpose that prevails. (Prov. 19:21)

Lord, thank you for the reminder that regardless of the poorly conceived plans of my kid's heart, your will prevails. I know that you are the author of all life and hope, and I am grateful that I can rest safely in the promise that you have a plan and it is good.

———————

There is a river whose streams make glad the city of God,
    the holy place where the Most High dwells.
God is within her, she will not fall;
    God will help her at break of day.
Nations are in uproar, kingdoms fall;
    he lifts his voice, the earth melts. (Ps 46:4–6)

Loving Father, my daughter is in trouble! She has turned away from you, making choices that will lead only to pain and sorrow. Lord, her life is in an uproar. I pray that you flow into her. Fill her with you so she cannot fall. Help her to break free of this trouble, and cover her with your love.

———————

You, Lord, are our Father.
    We are the clay, you are the potter;
    we are all the work of your hand. (Isa. 64:8)

O Great Potter, do a great work in my kids' lives. Make them and mold them into what you want them to be. I know that my kids are the great work of your hand, and I trust you with them, Lord. Give me the patience to see the big picture instead of just the tiny pieces I see right now.

———————

• • • • •

Prayers for Myself

From this time many of his disciples turned back and no longer followed him.

"You do not want to leave too, do you?" Jesus asked the Twelve.

Simon Peter answered him, "Lord, to whom shall we go? You have the words of eternal life." (John 6:66–68)

Lord Jesus, you have the words of eternal life. I vow today to stand next to you for the rest of my life. Lord, please help me to always point my child to you. Let me be an example of "I will stay! I will serve you!" because you are the only hope we have.

If you love me, keep my commands. And I will ask the Father, and he will give you another advocate to help you and be with you forever—the Spirit of truth. The world cannot accept him, because it neither sees him nor knows him. But you know him, for he lives with you and will be in you. (John 14:15–17)

Merciful Father, you say that if we love you, we will obey you. I want to obey you, but I confess that I also have a spirit of rebellion at times. I rebel against your truth not because it's not right or perfect but because I am of this world. Forgive me for my rebellion so I can be a beacon of light for my daughter.

Now fear the LORD and serve him with all faithfulness. Throw away the gods your ancestors worshiped beyond the Euphrates River and in Egypt, and serve the LORD. But if serving the LORD seems undesirable to you, then choose for yourselves this day whom you will serve, whether the gods your ancestors served beyond the Euphrates, or the gods of the Amorites, in whose land you are living. But as for me and my household, we will serve the LORD. (Josh. 24:14–15)

Father God, I choose this day and always to serve you. Regardless of the choices my kids make or the things that happen in our lives, I choose you. I pray, Lord, that you give me the tools I need to guide my entire household to a saving faith. Fill me with wisdom and patience and love so I know the right words to say at the right time.

9

when my child is running away from God

"There is a time in a child's life when they stray from their family's traditions and morals and wander away from God. It's called their twenties."

When my pastor, Scott Simmerok, said this, you could hear nervous giggles throughout the auditorium. And I knew who all those laughing people were: women with kids age twenty and older. No, not every child runs away from God. I had my own time in my late teens and early twenties when I wasn't exactly running away from him, but I certainly was running from his loving laws. I still longed for God's love, just not his rules. While at the time those felt like two different things, I've come to realize that you can't partition off God. You're either reaching toward him or running away.

Now my kids are in their twenties and I'm being forced to relive those same decisions through them. I would love to be done with this chapter, to be able to tie it all up with a nice red bow and tell you that while my kids ran away for a bit, they are now all loving God and living according to his principles. Sadly, that is not the case for all of my kids. I would love it if it were, not because I want the title of "good mom" (okay, I wouldn't hate that title), but because I know the pain that comes with living away from God. I want them to learn their lessons fast, come back to God, and live in peace. But even though that's what I want, from what I've seen that is rarely the road most of us take when it comes to following Jesus.

When My Child Is Running Away from God, I Feel Hopeless

When my husband, Roger, was a little kid, he was studying botany in elementary school and came across the word *heliotropism*, the process by which flowers—most famously sunflowers—follow the sun. Knowing that his mom was growing a sunflower in the backyard, Roger went outside to make sure that their sunflower was doing what it was supposed to be doing.

But when Roger got out there, he realized that their sunflower was not doing the right thing. Instead of turning toward the sun, their sunflower was stretching the complete opposite direction. It was straining toward a decorative lamp that was glowing in their yard.

Roger, even from a young age, was concerned that everyone—and everything—should be doing what they were supposed to be doing. Roger knew that the sunflower was supposed to be facing the sun (it was even implied in the name). So Roger took matters into his own hands. Literally. He stood up on his tippy-toes, and with his arm stretched high above his head, he reached up and turned that flower head toward the sun.

That would have been fine, except for the definitive *snap* that the sunflower made as it separated from its stalk.

Oh, friends. I have tried so many times to turn my kids in the right direction when it comes to God. I have forced them to attend church, I have guilted them into going to youth group, and I have taken matters into my own hands. Roger and I have talked until we are blue in the face about their relationship with God. We have tried, just like Roger and the sunflower, to force our kids in the right direction.

You may argue the merits of forced church attendance, family prayer, and so on. But here is the thing I've found: for some kids, those just don't work. They cause the kids to snap. And that's when our attempts at raising godly kids start to feel hopeless. Not for all kids, but some.

I have no idea where your child is going to land. I have no idea how God is going to woo your child back to him. But I do know this: almost every Christian I know and love—every man and woman who is now doing great things on behalf of the kingdom of God—has had a time of running away.

When My Child Is Running Away from God, I Feel Hopeless, but God Is My Shepherd

> For this is what the Sovereign LORD says: I myself will search for my sheep and look after them. As a shepherd looks after his scattered flock when he is with them, so will I look after my sheep. I will rescue them from all the places where they were scattered on a day of clouds and darkness. (Ezek. 34:11–12)

God knows not only when we are running from him but why. There is no place we can hide, there is no place we can go where we are out of his sight. God doesn't look around and then, when we aren't standing right in front of him, just give up. God says he is with us: "As a shepherd looks after his scattered flock when he is with them, so will I look after my sheep." God is not waiting for us or our kids to straighten up, fly right, and come back into the fold. He is looking after us, rescuing us.

There is no place God won't go to bring your child back. Yes, your child has free will; yes, your child can spend a lot of time and a lot of energy running away from God. But God will never give up pursuing your child. He loves your kid that much.

It's when we start putting our trust in the sheep and not the shepherd that we run into trouble.

We parents run a real danger of misplaced hope. We put our hope for our kids in our kids. We try to control their actions, their thoughts. We give them the best education available, take them to youth group, and invest our time and energy in them instead of committing them to God every single day.

It's like wanting to fly a kite. You invest in the best kite on the market and then trick it out: the best tail, the best reel, and the best string. You spend all your time on the kite and never bother to see if there is any wind. Our hope is in the wind—in Christ.

Instead of worrying about what you did or didn't do, instead of stopping your own life until your kids "get back on track," instead of putting your hope in your kids, put your hope in the only one who loves your kids more than you do. Put your hope in the only place it can make a difference.

A Story from the Trenches

I remember kneeling by my bed and asking Jesus into my heart as a child, begging God to come into my life. I remember getting baptized in front of the congregation, my mom proudly handing me a pink Bible with my name engraved in gold on the cover as I stepped out of the water. I remember summers and church camp, evenings at youth group, afternoons spent with my Young Life small group. I did all the right things and knew all the right words to say to be a "good Christian girl."

But my faith was lukewarm. It wasn't that I ever stopped believing in God, but simply that I had no passion, no heartfelt yearning to know him.

And so, when I went off to college, I started living a double life. I volunteered as a Young Life leader by day but drank and partied by night. I prayed and read my Bible on Sunday mornings but spent the rest of the week hanging out with friends, hardly thinking about God. I went through the motions for years, living a life that carefully trapped God in the box I wanted him to be in.

That all changed on September 11, 2001.

I was living in Costa Rica with my new husband, and we had woken up in our tiny hostel to hear the horrible news of that day. Reeling, terrified, and seemingly alone, my husband and I wandered out onto the beach, stumbling down a well-worn path, looking for something or someone to make sense of what was happening in our world. And God intervened.

As we walked, scared and alone, I earnestly prayed to God for the first time in years, begging him to comfort me, to give me a sign of hope, to bring me back to him. I remember a wind picking up, blowing through me. And the next thing I knew, a tiny yellow scrap of paper blew into my hand. It read, "Prayer meeting on the beach, 5 p.m. tonight." We went.

There on that isolated beach, we were surrounded by faithful Christians, a ragtag group of American missionaries and expatriates who prayed fervently for our country and for those lost. We prayed for repair and for hope and that God would use evil events for his own purposes. And for the first time in years, my heart felt full. Hopeful almost. Even in the midst of great tragedy.

That night, the missionaries leading the prayer vigil invited us into their home. They fed us—literally and figuratively—and showed us what it meant to live life as true servants of Christ.

When we got back to the States from Costa Rica, my husband and I made some big changes. We joined a church. We got involved in a small group. We started reading the Bible. And while I was certainly a Christian before, I can say that it was on that beach in Costa Rica that I stopped running away from God.

Erin MacPherson

Practical Steps

I think my number one tip for parents who watch their kids running away from God is to do the exact opposite of what you think you should do. I know the temptation well: you want to plead, to lecture, to hammer the idea of God into your kids' heads so they can't help but turn back to him. But as you're probably learning, that doesn't work. Here are my tips:

1. **Pray for God to intervene.** God loves your kids. He desires that they turn to him, that they honor him, that they glorify him. So you can rest assured that he is actively pursuing them. One thing I've done is pray that God intervenes in a big way in my kids' lives so they can't help but fall on their knees to honor him.

2. **Pray that God would surround your child.** In my time of walking away from God, every cool person in my life turned out to be a Christian, from the new salesgirl at work who I just adored to the guy who helped me pass my first year of college English. Pray that God would send people into your child's life who can speak truth to them in a way that—let's be honest—can be hard for a parent to do.

3. **Live a life worthy of the calling.** This probably goes without saying, but if you want your kids to stop running away from God, you have to set an example of what a godly life looks like. Roger and I work really hard to lead lives that reflect our faith. Although we know that things like going to church, reading the Bible every day, and praying continuously aren't necessary for our salvation, we also know that we are much more fulfilled when we do those things. We hope that our kids will see our joy and fulfillment and start to crave the same.

4. **Be ready for tough questions.** My friend Jamie told me that one day her college-age son Matthew called out of the blue and asked her, "Mom, if God is real, then why does he always

seem to abandon me when I need him most?" Gulp. Jamie said her first instinct was to argue with Matthew, to tell him that he was being crazy to ever doubt God. But then she realized this was her opportunity to share her faith with her son, who had run away from it. So she said a quick prayer and asked Matthew to explain what he meant by that statement. They had a really great talk that day. Matthew shared the pain of a recent falling-out with a girlfriend, and Jamie had the opportunity to share her own struggles and pain in a way that eventually led Matthew back to the God who would never disappoint him.

Be ready to answer tough questions with honesty and transparency. It's okay for your kids to see that you don't know everything, but show them that you do trust the nature of God in those circumstances where you don't understand.

5. **Be patient.** It's hard to watch our kids struggle with what should be the most important relationship in their lives. It's even more difficult when their struggle lasts for months or even years. Don't give up on your kids and their faith! Pray for them daily, even if it takes decades for them to come back.

6. **Trust God.** God will pursue your child. I've heard countless stories about God pursuing seemingly impossible people— people who have hardened their hearts, run away for years, and shunned God and his plans. But God loves his people. Even if it seems impossible, I urge you to trust him for your kid's salvation and return to him.

· · · · ·

Prayers for My Child

The Lord is not slow in keeping his promise, as some understand slowness. Instead he is patient with you, not wanting anyone to perish, but everyone to come to repentance. (2 Pet. 3:9)

Great Savior, you have promised us that you want everyone to come to repentance. I pray that you continue to seek my child even as he runs away from you. Father God, my heart aches for my child because I understand the joy that comes from knowing you. Stop him in his tracks and help him turn to you.

From inside the fish Jonah prayed to the LORD his God. He said:

"In my distress I called to the LORD,
    and he answered me.
From deep in the realm of the dead I called for help,
    and you listened to my cry.
You hurled me into the depths,
    into the very heart of the seas,
    and the currents swirled about me;
all your waves and breakers
    swept over me.
I said, 'I have been banished
    from your sight;
yet I will look again
    toward your holy temple.'
The engulfing waters threatened me,
    the deep surrounded me;
    seaweed was wrapped around my head.
To the roots of the mountains I sank down;
    the earth beneath barred me in forever.
But you, LORD my God,
    brought my life up from the pit." (Jon. 2:1–6)

Like Jonah, my child is running from you right now. She's decided that it's easier to sail away from Nineveh

124

than to follow your will. Lord, bring her up from the pit. Help her to see that the only life worth living is one that is through you. Protect her from evil as you pursue her, Lord.

Then the word of the LORD came to Jonah a second time: "Go to the great city of Nineveh and proclaim to it the message I give you."

Jonah obeyed the word of the LORD and went to Nineveh. Now Nineveh was a very large city; it took three days to go through it. Jonah began by going a day's journey into the city, proclaiming, "Forty more days and Nineveh will be overthrown." The Ninevites believed God. A fast was proclaimed, and all of them, from the greatest to the least, put on sackcloth. (Jon. 3:1–5)

Wonderful Savior, as Jonah turned back to you, I pray that you guide my child to do the same. When Jonah finally decided to turn toward you and away from sin, you chose not only to forgive him but to bless his ministry. Do the same for my child! Help him to turn back to you and then give him the passion, desire, and ability to make a big difference in your kingdom.

Where can I go from your Spirit?
　　Where can I flee from your presence?
If I go up to the heavens, you are there;
　　if I make my bed in the depths, you are there.
If I rise on the wings of the dawn,
　　if I settle on the far side of the sea,
even there your hand will guide me,
　　your right hand will hold me fast. (Ps. 139:7–10)

Holy God, my child cannot flee from you. You are so big, so great, so powerful that your mighty love stretches from the highest heavens to the depths of the sea. Lord, guide my child back to you—guide him with your gentle, loving hand back into the fold of your love.

● ● ● ● ●

Prayers for Myself

For since the creation of the world God's invisible qualities—his eternal power and divine nature—have been clearly seen, being understood from what has been made, so that people are without excuse. (Rom. 1:20)

God, I know that you speak for yourself. There is no need to convince my child of anything—your invisible qualities, eternal power, and divine nature say more than a million words. Please give me the courage to pray continuously, love fully, and trust wholly when it comes to my child.

Who shall separate us from the love of Christ? Shall trouble or hardship or persecution or famine or nakedness or danger or sword? As it is written:

"For your sake we face death all day long;
    we are considered as sheep to be slaughtered."

No, in all these things we are more than conquerors through him who loved us. For I am convinced that neither death nor life, neither angels nor demons, neither the present nor the future, nor any powers, neither height nor depth, nor anything else in all creation, will be able to separate us from the love of God that is in Christ Jesus our Lord. (Rom. 8:35–39)

Christ Jesus my Lord, there is nothing that can separate me from you. Nothing! Nothing in my world, nothing supernatural, not even my kids when they run away from you. What a wonderful promise! Even as my child wanders away from you, I pray that you fill me with your peace and mercy. Hold me tight so I am able to steadfastly seek your will in each of our lives. Your love is more powerful than anything! Thank you for giving me something I can believe in, trust in, and take comfort in.

10

when my child is lacking character

Justen has always been the kind of kid who has the motto, "Why stand when you can sit? Why sit when you can lie down? And why lie down if you can veg on the couch and tune out the world?"

It frustrates me to no end.

Justen, who is incredibly smart, would spend twice as long thinking about how to get out of doing a job than it would take to simply do it and get it over with. I suspected that he spent more time hiding out in his room pretending to be busy in order to avoid chores than he spent playing video games. Oh, how he hated work.

Okay, if I'm being honest, he does like some types of work. He loves working on the computer, loves writing, loves anything word related. But if it's a job that he doesn't like—say, when the cat box needs to be cleaned out—Justen is nowhere to be found.

Justen also has a lot of great personal qualities. He's really a great guy, and I'd say one day he'll make a great husband and dad. He has a soft spot for the elderly and animals, he is passionate about literature, and he's totally invested in the things he cares about.

But when it came to work, instead of putting his head down and plowing through, Justen was known to take the easy way out. And that became glaringly obvious when I married Roger and Justen's stepbrother, Jeremy, joined our household.

(A side note: Justen now pitches in around the house without grumbling or complaining—most of the time. But hey, who loves chores 100 percent of the time?)

When Jeremy realized he was the slowest guy on the high school track team, he didn't wallow in self-pity or quit track to take up theater. No, he ran every night until he could beat everyone else's time. When he played hockey, he asked his dad to take him to the rink even on non-practice days. (Since he weighed 110 pounds, it was important that Jeremy knew how to skate fast to avoid weekly concussions.)

Now, Jeremy has worked for the same company for six years. He started as a grocery bagger and worked his way to being a baker, and throughout the years he has shown up for work rain or shine, even when he was injured. He has even worked other people's shifts when they're sick. He has proven that his work ethic means he will always do his job well.

It's sometimes a bit hard for me not to compare kids—especially when they live in the same house and are close to the same age. One child would rather skip video game time than tell you a lie, and the other child lies as easily as a crooked lawyer with their fingers crossed behind them.

Maybe you know what your child's character weaknesses are— or maybe your child has done a great job hiding them. But the truth is that we're all human, and every human has—to put it very nicely—some major character flaws. As moms, all of us are going to make some ugly discoveries about our kids' issues. It's part of life, and I guarantee that it's going to happen.

I don't know about you, but to me it feels like a rip-off. I tried really hard to instill good character in my kids, and they still ended up doing ridiculous things.

Do you ever feel the same way? You feel like you've done all the right stuff—you took your kids to church every week and even did family devotions at home. You returned the extra money the checker gave you at the grocery store so she wouldn't get in trouble—but also to exemplify to your kids what honesty looks like. You raised your kids on *Adventures in Odyssey*, paid more than your fair share of taxes, and went out of your way to always be a person of character. And yet still there are days when the way you raised your kids doesn't match up with how they are acting.

That's what this chapter is about—not to go on and on bashing your kid's character but instead to help you see your kid for what he is: a fully flawed human whom God loves desperately. I can assure you that God will use your kid's character flaws to—you guessed it—grow character. And here's how you can help your kid as he does.

When My Child Is Lacking Character, I Feel Frustrated

Several years ago, I took some cooking lessons at a community college. I wanted to get better with my knife skills and understand a little of the science behind cooking. In the class, we made dozens of recipes and finally got to one I had been dying to try—Greek lemon soup. It was one of Justen's favorites, and I wanted to be able to whip it up for him for his next birthday.

Everyone in the class started off with the exact same ingredients and had the same set of instructions in front of us. But when our cooking time was over, my soup was sour (and not in the way it was supposed to be sour) and more than slightly inedible.

I was so incredibly frustrated. It just wasn't turning out the way I'd imagined it.

When the instructor and I did a postmortem on the dead soup, we went over each ingredient and instruction. I was able to tell her from memory exactly what I did to create the soup. All the while she was nodding approvingly, confirming each step along the way.

At the end of our discussion, she turned to me and said, "Kathi, you can do everything right. Sometimes the soup just doesn't turn out the way you want it to."

How's that for a spot-on example for motherhood? We may do all of the right things as moms—a dash of discipline here, a hefty dose of prayer there, a long afternoon of character education thrown in so our recipe will turn out perfectly. We can do all the right things and our kids still may not turn out the way we want them to.

Think back to your younger days. Were there character areas you struggled in? I know I had some huge character struggles. When I was a kid, and all the way up through my twenties, I enjoyed a loose interpretation of the truth. My reality was whatever I could get away with. It took the unconditional love of my Savior and my husband to make me realize that while my choices would hurt myself and others, those who truly cared about me would never stop loving me.

Whether you've lived a life you are proud of or have made some big mistakes along the way, I know one thing about you: you want kids of character. You've done your best to teach them right and wrong, given them consequences, and prayed that they would turn out all right. I also know how frustrating it is when all of your hard work and effort produce kids who do the exact things you've taught them not to do.

Frustrating, yes. But impossible? No. Our kids are works in progress. God loves them desperately and is using each of these character struggles to teach them—and (dare I say it?) us—about him.

When My Child Is Lacking Character, I Feel Frustrated, but God Encourages Me

When you pass through the waters,
   I will be with you;
and when you pass through the rivers,
   they will not sweep over you.
When you walk through the fire,
   you will not be burned;
the flames will not set you ablaze. (Isa. 43:2)

A friend of mine, Susan, just got into a minor car accident. She was stopped at a stoplight and had glanced into the backseat to talk to her kids, and the next thing she knew she felt a small bump. Susan had no idea how it happened—she had her foot firmly on the brake and couldn't imagine how she had hit the car in front of her—but she figured she must have accidentally let her foot slip off the brake while talking to her kids.

She put her car in park and got out. She glanced at her fender and saw what she expected—absolutely no damage to her car. It had been such a minor bump that she figured the worst-case scenario was just a scratch. But then Susan looked at the other car. Its entire fender was crushed. The trunk was hanging open, twisted and unable to close. The taillights were both crushed. And the man in the car got out holding his back, screaming that he was in incredible pain.

The man called 911, ranting about the horrible accident he was in and the amount of pain he was suffering. Police cars and ambulances came. Insurance adjustors speculated. People glared. And the whole time, Susan wondered how in the world such a small bump had turned into this crazy scene.

It dawned on her that perhaps this was fraud when she heard the man calling in sick to work, saying he had been in a horrible accident. Susan mentioned it to a police officer, and after some scrutiny they found the smoking gun: there was blue paint all over the fender of the other car. Susan's car was red.

The truth came out. The man had gotten into another accident—one that was his fault and not covered by his insurance. He had noticed Susan turn around, so he had gently put his car into reverse and bumped into her. And then the theatrics began.

Susan was so frustrated. It is frustrating to know you've done everything right—kept your cell phone in your purse while driving, kept your eye on the road, kept your foot on the brake—and to still have everything go so, so wrong. But as I reminded her, God is faithful. The crazy car accident guy didn't get away with his scheme, and the truth is neither will your kids.

God has proven his faithfulness again and again in the Bible. The best part about God's faithfulness is that he is faithful even when we aren't. Think about Abraham's wife Sarah (see Gen. 16–17). She desperately wanted a baby. She prayed and waited and waited and prayed, and finally she decided to take matters into her own hands. She had her handmaiden sleep with her husband in order to conceive a child, and then, once it was all done, she treated her handmaiden horribly out of spite and jealousy. Talk about lacking character!

But God didn't give up on Sarah. He stayed with her. He molded her. He refined her. And finally, when she was past childbearing years, he gave her the gift that he had been planning all along: a son.

Likewise, God isn't going to give up on your kids. Regardless of the ridiculous things they do, he still loves them and is still completing a good work in them. He will use these learning experiences to refine them into men and women of noble character.

A Story from the Trenches

We all learned a tough lesson in car school last week. (A close relative of homeschool, *car school* is fifteen minutes of random "learning" in the car.)

To my children's great delight, I brought a snack when I picked them up from school. A snack during car school meant they wouldn't have to endure those excruciating fifteen minutes of hunger pangs between school and home. As a special treat, puffcorn was on the menu. Although my three boys *love* puffcorn, I'm not convinced it's actually food. I suspect the company salts the packing peanuts from their shipping department and bags them up to sell for just two dollars a bag. Even so, the boys were elated about their salted Styrofoam snack!

The bag was opened, and the aroma of artificial butter filled our vehicle. While his big brothers dug into the bag, my youngest son, Levi, who chose the unfortunate seat in our vehicle's third row, was tormented by the tantalizing smell and the soft crunching in the second row.

He was hollering for his brothers to hurry up and pass some back, and in an admirable effort to give Levi exactly what he wanted, my oldest poured a generous portion of puffcorn into an empty donut-hole container. (Now you know two things about me: I sometimes feed my kids ultra junk food, and I rarely clean out my vehicle.) Then he tossed the container back to his salivating brother.

But when Levi saw the donut-hole container filled with puffcorn come flying over the seat, he swatted it back like an ace at the net. He did *not* want his puffcorn in a second-rate container! No, he wanted the real bag, the one with the word "puffcorn"!

I couldn't decide whether to laugh, get angry, or lecture. So naturally I did all three.

First, I laughed. Levi had legitimately spiked a donut-hole container filled with puffcorn through the vehicle, and amazingly it did not spill.

Second, I got angry. Levi had been clamoring for puffcorn! Realizing it was going to be a back-and-forth deal all the way home, his big brother had tried to solve the problem. He gave Levi exactly what he wanted and needed—a generous portion of that satisfying snack. But Levi smacked it back because he didn't like the container.

Finally I gave a loud and impatient lecture. "Hey! Don't complain about the container. It's the same puffcorn! Stop pouting about the container, and be thankful that you got exactly what you wanted."

Humph!

Then two seconds after he accepted the puffcorn-packed container, I looked in the rearview mirror and realized maybe the lecture should have been for me.

On a level that doesn't involve junk food, I have complained about the container.

I have asked God for a generous portion of patience. But instead of handing me a celestial gift, he's packaged it in the form of some young and at times impatient human beings. Sometimes I don't care for that kind of packaging, and I swat it back at him. Like a demanding brat, I whine, "That's not how I wanted it!" But when I bump up against humans and practice a patient response, my "patience muscle" gets a little bit stronger. And I realize he's given exactly what I needed.

Other times I've asked God to supply all our needs. But instead of padding our pockets, he's given the gift of digging deep until only pocket lint remains. Like a spoiled child, I hurl a lint-covered accusation at him. And when I hang my head in disappointment, I see the shoes on my feet grinding crumbs into the carpet—evidence that we have been clothed, housed, and fed. And I realize he's given exactly what I needed.

So instead of puffcorn, I've been snacking on humble pie. It's not as tasty as it sounds, and I don't really care for the packaging. But as I peek into my own entitled heart, not surprisingly, it has been exactly what I needed.

Shauna Letellier

Practical Steps

It's easy to start feeling like anything but mom of the year when your kids' character flaws begin to show. Here are some easy ways to look beyond the behavior to the heart of the issue:

1. **Don't let shame drive you.** I remember feeling so ashamed— yes, ashamed—when I watched Roger's son, Jeremy, head

off to work all prompt and perfect while it was an effort to drag my son out of bed in the morning to do . . . well, anything. Had I failed as a mom? Had I not done enough character education? But after some prayer and thought (okay, and a lot of reassurance from my sweet and brilliant husband), I realized that my shame was just that—shame. A human emotion that did nothing good other than to make me feel awful. The truth is that God has created each of us—Justen, Jeremy, me—with a specific set of unique characteristics and for a purpose. Being ashamed of someone else's character is kind of like telling God that he didn't do something right.

2. **Don't overlook the good.** Shame can cause you to overlook the really, really great characteristics that your kids have. Take Justen, for example. He is truly an elderly-whisperer. I know that's not a real thing, but put him in a room at a nursing home and he will have every man and woman in that room regaling him with tales of the good old days. They love him! And it's because they feel respected and honored by him—he listens attentively and smiles naturally. But if Justen was the next Gordon Gekko—only wondering where his next dollar was coming from, so focused on his job he couldn't see the people around him—he wouldn't be the kind of guy he is. And so when you see areas of character lacking in your kids, yes, address them, but also look for the silver linings to even the darkest clouds.

3. **Don't lecture.** My friend Sarah tends to be a little flighty. Okay, so she's a lot flighty. But I adore her in spite of it. She spent yesterday morning searching for her cell phone, which she had lost for the 543rd time this week. After hours of searching, she found it in the pantry in the Cheerios box (because that's where cell phones go, you know), and she called her husband and triumphantly told him the news. He responded by very kindly and gently reminding her that if

she put her cell phone in a designated place, it wouldn't get lost. Oh, and if she got the iPhone finder, she'd be able to find it anyway.

Sarah burst into tears. You see, she knows she's flighty. She knows she's irresponsible with her cell phone. But the last thing she needs to hear from her husband is a lecture about it. Same with your kids. As easy as it is to want to lecture them about good character, oftentimes a lecture will only serve to aggravate instead of to encourage. Instead, pray, teach, and pray some more.

4. **Trust God to work in your child's life.** Remember that soup story? I had done everything right to make the perfect Greek lemon soup, but it still turned out bad. I have to say, kids are like Greek lemon soup. You can follow the recipe for good parenting perfectly, but sometimes they might not turn out exactly like you want them to. Trust God to give your kids the challenges they need to grow the character he wants.

. . . . .

Prayers for My Child

Enter through the narrow gate. For wide is the gate and broad is the road that leads to destruction, and many enter through it. But small is the gate and narrow the road that leads to life, and only a few find it. (Matt. 7:13–14)

Father God, I want my kids to follow you. Desperately. But in this crazy world, sometimes it's hard. I know that the ways of the world lead to destruction, so I pray that you show my kids that the easy way isn't the right way. Show them clearly that while following you may be difficult at times, it always leads to life.

Submit yourselves, then, to God. Resist the devil, and he will flee from you. Come near to God and he will come near to you. (James 4:7–8)

Jesus, give my kids the courage to submit to you and what is good and to flee from the devil and what is evil. Draw my kids close to you, Lord, and never let them go.

Likewise, every good tree bears good fruit, but a bad tree bears bad fruit. A good tree cannot bear bad fruit, and a bad tree cannot bear good fruit. Every tree that does not bear good fruit is cut down and thrown into the fire. Thus, by their fruit you will recognize them. (Matt. 7:17–20)

In the Bible, it's very clear that following you produces spiritual fruit. Lord, light a fire in my kids to do what's right. Help them to produce sweet spiritual fruit in their lives so you and your kingdom will be honored.

Therefore, I urge you, brothers and sisters, in view of God's mercy, to offer your bodies as a living sacrifice, holy and pleasing to God—this is your true and proper worship. Do not conform to the pattern of this world, but be transformed by the renewing of your mind. Then you will be able to test and approve what God's will is—his good, pleasing and perfect will. (Rom. 12:1–2)

Merciful God, I can't choose for my kids. I can't make them holy and pleasing to you. I can't force them to

139

worship you. But I can pray that you will fill them with your Spirit so they will be transformed, not by the craziness of our world but by you, the one who has a perfect plan for their lives.

· · · · ·

Prayers for Myself

God's love has been poured out into our hearts through the Holy Spirit, who has been given to us.

You see, at just the right time, when we were still power-less, Christ died for the ungodly. (Rom. 5:5–6)

Loving Father, it is hard to watch my kids choose the wrong way. I know they will suffer for it. But I also know your Word says you died for the ungodly. For the lost, the hurt, the needy, the hopeless. I know my kids are included in that promise. Thank you for your great love for your children!

That, however, is not the way of life you learned when you heard about Christ and were taught in him in accordance with the truth that is in Jesus. You were taught, with regard to your former way of life, to put off your old self, which is being corrupted by its deceitful desires; to be made new in the attitude of your minds; and to put on the new self, created to be like God in true righteousness and holiness. (Eph. 4:20–24)

Christ Jesus, I know the truth. I know you are the truth and the only path to life. Lord, help me to reject my

140

old self and to renew my mind so I can be everything you want me to be. I know you desire righteousness and holiness from me, and I know only through you is that possible. Without you, we are all lost. I ask you to come into my life in a powerful and loving way and show me your will.

"Very truly I tell you Pharisees, anyone who does not enter the sheep pen by the gate, but climbs in by some other way, is a thief and a robber. The one who enters by the gate is the shepherd of the sheep. The gatekeeper opens the gate for him, and the sheep listen to his voice. He calls his own sheep by name and leads them out. When he has brought out all his own, he goes on ahead of them, and his sheep follow him because they know his voice. But they will never follow a stranger; in fact, they will run away from him because they do not recognize a stranger's voice." Jesus used this figure of speech, but the Pharisees did not understand what he was telling them. (John 10:1–6)

Lord God, protect me. I know that in this world there are Pharisees, thieves, and robbers. There are people who would encourage me, even as a mom, to do the wrong thing, to live a life that's not worthy of you. Lord, be my gatekeeper. Give me an innate desire to associate with people who speak your glory. Give me an ear to hear your Word as the sweet music it is and a heart that rejects untruth.

The LORD your God will circumcise your hearts and the hearts of your descendants, so that you may love him with all your heart and with all your soul, and live. (Deut. 30:6)

O God, you have promised that you will mercifully pour out your love and salvation on all who choose you. Fill me with a desire for you and you alone so that everything I say and everything I do honors you. I pray that you do what you have to so you'll have my heart and the hearts of those I love.

11

when my child is struggling

Another doctor.

Another doctor telling me I'm crazy.

There I was with Justen, trying to get to the root of his problems—our problems. But every time I took him to see a specialist, Justen acted as if there was nothing wrong. He put on a mask and used everything he learned in theater class to feed into the notion that I was a mom who was overly worried, and if I would learn to just chill out, everything would be fine.

But it wasn't fine.

The hole in the wall at the top of our stairs said it wasn't fine.

The door slamming and foot stomping all over the house said it wasn't fine.

Every member of our household, including the dog, being on guard for the outbursts all the time said it wasn't fine.

I've asked Justen if I could share this part of our lives with you. He understands that it's messy. He understands that there is a stigma attached to depression. But his bravery is just one of the many things that I admire about him—and he has given me permission to share this part of our family.

There is a worse place to be in than knowing your child has emotional issues. It's the place where you know it—your whole family knows it—but no one seems able to help.

We went through years of trying to get Justen the diagnosis and the help he needed. Finally, after eight long years, we have a doctor's slip of paper with a diagnosis code, another slip with a prescription, and a therapist who is making huge strides in helping Justen cope in life. But it was a long road getting to this place—and the journey isn't over.

Every day we see a little more of who Justen really is. Every day we see more of his humor and caring coming out. Every day Justen's health—and our family—heals a little bit more.

I'm proud of Justen. So many kids struggle emotionally and are stuck—and their stuck parents and families are right there with them. Justen was stuck for a long time, but even though it's uncomfortable, he is taking steps and doing the things he needs to get healthy. He's taking medication (after trying several that didn't work), he's exercising, and he's hanging out with friends again. To some parents, those may seem like nothing. To us? Justen is a walking miracle.

Maybe you are walking in my shoes. Perhaps you are worried about your teen who seems to have an emotional crisis every day. Or maybe there is a family legacy of mental illness and it keeps you up at night as you worry about what the future looks like for your child. It could even be that your adult child has been diagnosed with anxiety or depression and you see no hope for their future.

The first thing you need to know is that you're not alone. I speak all over the country, and when I finally started talking about the emotional health of our families at some of my weekend-long events, the floodgates were thrown wide open. Countless women have shared their stories. Stories about a bright, gifted son who was trapped in the grips of depression. Or about a daughter whose diary described in detail how she would kill herself. Or about the child who seemed to have given up on life.

These are real stories, and they are happening in many families. Real kids have real problems that are tearing them apart inside and tearing them from the ones they need most: God, family, and friends. It's painful. But it's not hopeless. I know from personal experience that there is something powerful we can do when our kids are struggling emotionally. Prayer and action are a powerful combination.

Whatever the issues—whether anxiety, depression, or something else—we must keep prayer at the forefront of our strategies in dealing with them, for both our child and ourselves.

There are also another hundred things we need to do as parents when our child is suffering emotionally. Our child needs treatment. Our child needs doctors who understand that this may not be just a phase. And we need to remember that our child and their issues are not the same thing.

Pastor Rick Warren, whose son Matthew committed suicide when he was twenty-seven years old, said to those who are suffering from mental illness, "Your illness is not your identity, your chemistry is not your character."[4] That truth can be hard to separate—your beautiful baby and the unreasonable behaviors; the creative, sensitive child and the chaotic ups and downs. All of it is maddening (because mental illness is so maddening) and tricky.

When My Child Is Struggling, I Feel Anxious

If your child is struggling, I know it's a lonely place. It is a rare church that has a group for the families of those who struggle emotionally. I get it—there may not be a lot of people who stand up and say, "My kid is suffering and I don't know what to do." But then the isolation leads to shame, and the shame leads to more isolation, until you feel like you are the only person who is going through this and somehow it must be your fault—there must be something you did or didn't do for your child to be this way. And the cycle continues.

This whole cycle of emotions—shame, blame, guilt—is based in fear. When a child is struggling with emotional issues, it's easy to give in to the fear every day. *Will my child be okay? What if we can't find the right medication? What if we can't get the right diagnosis? What if I can't help him?*

These are real questions, and they cause real anxiety in us and our families. I hate mental illness in the way that I hate cancer. The anxiety it brings to those who suffer from it—and those who love them—is as real as if you could reach out and touch it.

When My Child Is Struggling, I Feel Anxious, but God Is My Peace

Rejoice in the Lord always. I will say it again: Rejoice! Let your gentleness be evident to all. The Lord is near. Do not be anxious about anything, but in every situation, by prayer and petition, with thanksgiving, present your requests to God. And the peace of God, which transcends all understanding, will guard your hearts and your minds in Christ Jesus.

Finally, brothers and sisters, whatever is true, whatever is noble, whatever is right, whatever is pure, whatever is lovely, whatever is admirable—if anything is excellent or praiseworthy—think about such things. Whatever you have learned or received or heard from me, or seen in me—put it into practice. And the God of peace will be with you. (Phil. 4:4–9)

I used to pray daily for Justen to get the help he needed. My prayer was, "God, I just want peace in our home!" And I did want that, but now I realize that what I really wanted for all those years was for Justen to just be okay. I wanted his problems to go away. I wanted to live in a home where the doors weren't slammed, no one yelled at each other, and my ugly side didn't come out on a regular basis. I wanted to not be confronted every single day with the pain and the heartache. I wanted healing for Justen, but I also wanted peace for myself and the rest of my family.

It's situations like mine that make it crystal clear how important it is for us all to take Philippians 4:6–7 to heart: "Do not be anxious about anything, but in every situation, by prayer and petition, with thanksgiving, present your requests to God. And the peace of God, which transcends all understanding, will guard your hearts and your minds in Christ Jesus."

God is not saying, "Just stop worrying!" He is saying, "Here are the real steps to peace in every situation: Pray. Ask me to show you my will. Thank me for what I am going to do in this situation. Tell me what you want. And when you do this, my peace, which is so much more than you will ever understand, will guard your heart and your mind in my power."

It's interesting to me that the Bible never promises healing for everyone. God could heal everyone who prayed, but he knows that's not always best. God does promise peace, though. He promises a peace that surpasses all understanding for each and every person who seeks him and trusts him. And that is what I am doing— trusting God in this situation with Justen. I don't know what our next step is. I have no guarantee that Justen will continue with his medication. I have no promise of healing. But God does promise that he loves me and he loves Justen.

A Story from the Trenches

Fear is a powerful thing. It can keep us immobilized, unable to make a decision, making it impossible for us to help our child who is in pain.

Fellow author Cheri Gregory shares about how she moved from immobilizing fear to real help for her daughter Annemarie:

> "I went to the counseling center on campus. I even started filling out the paperwork to see a therapist."

Annemarie, now a college senior, is remembering back to her freshman year.

"But when I got to the question that said, 'Are you considering killing yourself?' I stopped, left, and never went back." Mascara-stained tears draw dark lines down her cheeks as she pauses to compose herself. "I didn't check the 'Yes' box because I didn't want to admit the truth, Mom. Not to them. Not to you. Not to myself."

My tears flow freely as I listen. I fight the clamor of inner thoughts to stay focused on my daughter. But accusations surface anyway.

How did I not know?

Why didn't I sense that things had gotten this serious?

How did I let this happen to her?

Reading my mind—we often joke about our mother-daughter "mind meld"—Annemarie continues.

"I worked so hard to protect you, Mom. I hid the truth about how bad things had gotten from everyone. I didn't want you to know because I didn't want you to worry about me. Then—and I know how crazy this sounds now—I was mad and hurt that you didn't come help me." She wipes her eyes. "I thought you didn't care. But you didn't even know."

I didn't even know.

My daughter almost killed herself.

And I didn't even know.

I recall a news story that gave me nightmares for months. A beautiful, bright, outgoing college girl—who sounded so much like my Annemarie—had walked out of the campus counseling center to get lunch but never returned. After a month of searching, the girl's own mother found her daughter's body; she had hung herself from a tree. I could only begin to imagine the torment of guilt and grief that poor mother felt.

I didn't lose my daughter, but I am still assaulted by answerless questions.

Why?

What did I do wrong?

Why?

148

We've processed Annemarie's depression as a family, with the help of two excellent counselors, lots of honest dialogue, and ongoing prayer. We've learned some vital lessons that I hope will help other families struggling with similar issues and perhaps prevent unnecessary suffering.

Cheri Gregory

Practical Steps

This is one of the hardest tip sections for me to work on. Partly because it's so close to my heart, as I've dealt with it in my own family, and partly because I feel somewhat inadequate. I haven't always known what to do, and there are times I still don't. But I do want to come beside you, mom to aching mom, because I know how hard it is on moms when our kids are struggling emotionally. Mental illness advocate Kevin Breel says, "We live in a world where if you break your arm, everyone runs over to sign your cast, but if you admit you suffer from depression, everyone runs the other way."[5]

I've felt exactly like he does, like everyone is running away just because I'm talking about depression or emotional illness. I don't want to do that to you. So I've worked with Cheri to come up with a list of things that have helped us as moms deal with the overwhelming situation of a child who is struggling emotionally:

1. **Don't expect your child's experiences to mirror your own.**
   While Cheri couldn't wait to get out of the house and finally be free, her daughter Annemarie felt safe at home and worried about being away from family. She was apprehensive and intimidated by college, yet when she tried to share her fears, Cheri admitted she dismissed her daughter's words as just nerves and failed to hear her heart.
   As for me, when I was twenty-one I was living in Japan

as a missionary—every single day was a huge adventure for me—and that's what I hoped for my kids as well. But Justen was not remotely prepared for an experience like that, and instead of being disappointed, I needed to understand that was not the way Justen was going to live his life.

2. **Don't ignore the warning signs.** I let doctors convince me that I was just an overreacting mom. But these doctors didn't live at our house. I finally got smart and started to bring my husband along when I went to these doctor appointments. Roger is logical and plainspoken, and Justen couldn't deny it when two of us were saying how hard things were. He was forced to face up to the situation.

Cheri had her own set of warning signals for her daughter: *She seems to be sick a lot. She says she's studying all the time, but her grades aren't showing it. She tells me I expect too much of her, that everyone is struggling. Maybe times have changed since I was in college.* In every case, Cheri found it all too easy to rationalize away the warning signals. And while that eased her anxiety, it didn't help her daughter.

3. **Pay attention to family history.** Cheri suffered from an eating disorder throughout high school and was hospitalized for six weeks before starting college. Along with anorexia nervosa and bulimia, she was diagnosed as narcissistic and depressed. With these labels came extreme shame. She desperately wanted to leave them behind and not pass them along to her children.

Annemarie's father became severely depressed and suicidal and suffered a near breakdown after the death of his own father. Others in his family struggle with mood disorders.

And recently, Cheri has learned that her own mother has suffered from clinical depression her entire life.

Depression is a family legacy we need to address, not sweep under the carpet and hope nobody will notice. When we fail to address the impact in our family history and in our own experience, our kids will feel alone and defective while they are struggling, sure that nobody else could possibly understand what they are going through.

4. **Accept the truth and move to support it.** Say to yourself, "My child suffers from depression."

   We want better for our kids than we had for ourselves. But the only gift that we can truly give them is our support, understanding, and prayers—and that comes first from acceptance.

5. **Set clear boundaries and hold to them.** Work with a counselor to understand what behaviors are acceptable and when you need to intervene. When you're the parent of someone suffering with emotional issues, it's hard to know when you are being controlling, codependent, enabling, or helpful.

   When it was obvious that Justen wasn't taking his medication, our counselor said, "Well, I guess you'll have to watch him take it for a while." Oh, that just felt so wrong, but it was absolutely the right thing to do. Once he was back on his medications, we could have real conversations with him again about his health and healing.

6. **Listen.** Cheri admits that one of the hardest lessons she's learned is that she can listen without fixing. She says, "For so long, I was only willing to listen to what I thought I could fix. And since I knew I couldn't fix anything as serious as depression, I didn't want to listen. But Annemarie has always relied on me to be a sounding board for her, to help her clarify her thinking just by listening and asking occasional questions, perhaps sharing my own experience. When I shut down around the topic of depression, Annemarie's sense of isolation and shame intensified."

. . . . .

Prayers for My Child

"For I know the plans I have for you," declares the LORD, "plans to prosper you and not to harm you, plans to give you hope and a future." (Jer. 29:11)

Lord God, you have plans for my child! Perfect plans, hopeful plans. I pray that my child is able to continue to hope in you and your love even through difficult times.

For you created my inmost being;
    you knit me together in my mother's womb.
I praise you because I am fearfully and wonderfully made;
    your works are wonderful,
    I know that full well. (Ps. 139:13–14)

My Creator, my God, it's so comforting to know that you created my children just the way they are and with a plan in mind. I praise you because my children are fearfully and wonderfully made. Use them to do great things!

Therefore, since we have been justified through faith, we have peace with God through our Lord Jesus Christ, through whom we have gained access by faith into this grace in which we now stand. And we boast in the hope of the glory of God. Not only so, but we also glory in our sufferings, because we know that suffering produces perseverance; perseverance, character; and character, hope. And hope does not put us to shame, because God's love has been poured out into our hearts through the Holy Spirit, who has been given to us. (Rom. 5:1–5)

Father God, you have justified my kids through faith, and I pray that you now fill each of them with your peace. It's so easy to get caught up in the terrible things of this world—depression, suffering, sadness—but the truth is that by your grace, none of those things can bind us. Even as my child struggles emotionally, I pray that suffering will produce perseverance, character, and hope. Thank you for pouring out your love on my child.

Therefore, there is now no condemnation for those who are in Christ Jesus, because through Christ Jesus the law of the Spirit who gives life has set you free from the law of sin and death. For what the law was powerless to do because it was weakened by the flesh, God did by sending his own Son in the likeness of sinful flesh to be a sin offering. And so he condemned sin in the flesh, in order that the righteous requirement of the law might be fully met in us, who do not live according to the flesh but according to the Spirit. (Rom. 8:1–4)

Christ Jesus, we live in a world full of condemnation. People are cruel, unjust, unkind. But you have set us free! You alone have the power to set my child free, and I pray that you do exactly that. Heal the emotional hurts she is suffering. Comfort her with a peace that goes beyond understanding. Raise her up as a beacon for your kingdom in a way that shows the world how great you are.

I was given a thorn in my flesh, a messenger of Satan, to torment me. Three times I pleaded with the Lord to take it away from me. But he said to me, "My grace is sufficient for you, for my power is made perfect in weakness."

Therefore I will boast all the more gladly about my weaknesses, so that Christ's power may rest on me. That is why, for Christ's sake, I delight in weaknesses, in insults, in hardships, in persecutions, in difficulties. For when I am weak, then I am strong. (2 Cor. 12:7–10)

Great Healer, I pray that if it's in your will, remove this affliction from my child's life. Heal him from his emotional illness. Protect him from depression, anxiety, and hopelessness. But if it's not your will, I still know that your power is made perfect in our weakness, so I pray that your power hovers over my child. Fill him with your strength so your Spirit can work in great ways through our struggles.

• • • • •

Prayers for Myself

You will keep in perfect peace
    those whose minds are steadfast,
    because they trust in you. (Isa. 26:3)

O Holy Father, I trust in you. Fill me with your perfect peace.

For though we live in the world, we do not wage war as the world does. The weapons we fight with are not the weapons of the world. On the contrary, they have divine power to demolish strongholds. We demolish arguments and every pretension that sets itself up against the knowledge of God, and we take captive every thought to make it obedient to

Christ. And we will be ready to punish every act of disobedience, once your obedience is complete. (2 Cor. 10:3–6)

Lord, help me not to wage war on my child's emotional struggles the way someone of the world would. Help me to trust not in the rationalizations and ways of the world but in you. Give me wisdom to seek the right help, the right medication, the right doctors, the right therapists, and the right prayer warriors so all strongholds in my child's life and my own can be destroyed.

———————

You, then, why do you judge your brother or sister? Or why do you treat them with contempt? For we will all stand before God's judgment seat. It is written:

"'As surely as I live,' says the Lord,
'every knee will bow before me;
    every tongue will acknowledge God.'"

So then, each of us will give an account of ourselves to God. (Rom. 14:10–12)

Father God, give me a spirit of acceptance and love instead of judgment. Help me to see others as you see them: wholly imperfect but perfectly loved. I know that you are my mighty God and you have rescued me from powerful enemies, and I pray that as my child struggles, I'll be transparent with my own struggles so you can work in his life.

———————

You prepare a table before me
    in the presence of my enemies.
You anoint my head with oil;
    my cup overflows.

155

Surely your goodness and love will follow me
all the days of my life,
and I will dwell in the house of the LORD forever. (Ps. 23:5–6)

O Father, these emotional struggles are an enemy in our lives. But you have given us everything we need to overcome them. Lord, anoint me and my loved ones with your presence so our cups can overflow with your goodness. Thank you for being enough for each of us.

The LORD is my shepherd, I lack nothing.
He makes me lie down in green pastures,
he leads me beside quiet waters,
he refreshes my soul.
He guides me along the right paths
for his name's sake.
Even though I walk
through the darkest valley,
I will fear no evil,
for you are with me;
your rod and your staff,
they comfort me. (Ps. 23:1–4)

Loving Shepherd, there is nothing I need but you. I turn over my child's emotional struggles and my own to the one who refreshes my soul. Guide me along the right paths and fill me with a spirit of peace. Comfort me and my child even in our struggles, because I know our days of struggling are numbered. I trust in you, O God.

12

when my child is left out

"What is the hardest part of your parenting journey so far?"

I asked that question on my Facebook page, and many of the answers I got are represented in each of the chapters of this book, but two categories stood out among all the others as the hardest for parents: when our kids make poor choices and when others shut our kids out.

When I was in fourth grade, my family moved across town and I switched schools. At my new elementary school, I was assigned a buddy—someone to show me the ins and outs and to introduce me around. I've long since forgotten her name (or perhaps I've blocked it out), but let's call her Valerie.

I was assigned a seat next to Valerie in class, and it was her job to make sure that I knew important stuff like where the bathroom was, what table we were supposed to sit at during lunch, and all the other intricacies that the average fourth grader needed to navigate.

I was thrilled to have Valerie. I had been dreading facing my first recess alone, so I was relieved to hear I'd have a built-in friend. There is nothing worse than being on the playground, not knowing where to stand, and waiting for someone to be desperate enough for another player in four square to invite you over. So when the recess bell rang, I immediately jumped up next to Valerie and followed her outside.

But as I tagged along behind her, she looked at me with disdain in her eyes, wrinkled her nose, and sneered, "Go away, Fatty Kathi. No one wants you."

Yeah. Guess how many thousands of dollars Little Miss Valerie has cost me in therapy?

When My Child Is Left Out, I Feel Brokenhearted

If you had a similar experience in your formative years, watching your kids face rejection can have a double sting—you know intimately what your child is going through at that moment, but you also know the extra burden that can linger because of the thoughtlessness of a nine-year-old.

Whenever I saw one of my kids being left out, my heart ached. I was screaming mad as well. I didn't know I was capable of wishing boils on a mean nine-year-old, but apparently my brain was totally ready to go there.

When my friends on Facebook poured out their stories of their children being isolated, left out, ostracized, and alone, there was one word that the moms used over and over again to describe the feeling of watching their child not be a part of things: brokenhearted.

I get it. As moms, we would pay any amount of money and take on any sort of pain ourselves not to see our kids go through loneliness. And whether it's the subtle snub of a kindergarten classmate or all the way to harassment and bullying, it's painful.

I've learned that bullying and meanness and social isolation are the power plays of broken and hurting children who feel powerless in other areas of their lives and feel the need to exert some control over those they see as weak or different. It's okay for us to feel sorry for the kids who are mean to other kids—we don't know what their home lives are like. But we also need to be okay with taking every action we can to protect our own kids from these negative influences.

When My Child Is Left Out, I Feel Brokenhearted, but God Is with Us

> The LORD is close to the brokenhearted
> and saves those who are crushed in spirit. (Ps. 34:18)

When Justen was in elementary school, a little boy in his class—we'll call him Mean Boy—put a target on Justen's back. Mean Boy made life miserable for Justen on a regular basis. He kept him from playing with the other kids, picked on him, and called him names. And since he was almost a year older than Justen, Mean Boy towered over him and physically intimidated him in every way.

I went to his teacher and then finally to the pastor who was over the school. His response? "If your child getting picked on is the worst thing in your life, count yourself blessed."

Sadly, at that time I was a young mom who felt that everyone knew more about parenting than I did. I was unsure of my own decisions, and I felt that if the pastor thought I was overreacting, I must be.

But as I prayed, I felt God giving me clear direction. *Move Justen. Get him out of there.*

Ugh. I didn't want to cause waves. Maybe this child would stop bullying Justen if I just prayed more. But the thought of my little boy being tormented was too much. Even though those at the school thought I was overreacting, I couldn't leave him there. I knew there was another school in town that took bullying very seriously. But I also knew they had no openings.

And what about my car pool? I didn't want to leave the other mom out to dry. She was driving her four boys all over town to different schools, and if I bailed on her, her whole delicate system would crumble. So I kept praying.

Not long after my conversation with the pastor, my car pool sister in arms came to me and said, "I hate to do this to you, but there are some openings at the school I've wanted to get my son into. I need to make this change for him. I'm so sorry." The school he would be going to? The same one I wanted for Justen and Kimberly.

After running over to the school, filling out tons of paperwork, and requesting that their school files be transferred, I enrolled my kids in the new school. I pulled Justen out of his old school and kept him at home with me for a week so he would never have to see Mean Boy again.

Even though my friends at the old school thought I was blowing it out of proportion and others at the school thought Justen's problem would blow over, I had to help him. I finally realized I had to stop listening to others and start listening to God.

Our very first step is to understand that during a tough time—a lonely time or a misunderstood time—God is with us and, even more significantly, with our children. We need to be listening to and leaning on him.

When I need to remind myself that this isn't about me or my child "toughening up" or "being strong," two of the verses I cling to aren't about strength or tenacity but instead are about clinging to God when we feel alone:

No one will be able to stand against you all the days of your life. As I was with Moses, so I will be with you; I will never leave you nor forsake you. (Josh. 1:5)

Have I not commanded you? Be strong and courageous. Do not be afraid; do not be discouraged, for the LORD your God will be with you wherever you go. (Josh. 1:9)

I love what my friend Karey said when it comes to this struggle: "When my daughter Kasey was in fifth grade and was being ostracized by some of the other girls, she was eating alone for a period of time. It was really hard not to jump in and go eat with her every day but instead to trust God to grow her through the situation."

A Story from the Trenches

I played basketball my freshman year of high school.

By "played basketball," I mean I sat on the bench and occasionally got to go into the game to fumble around if my team was ahead by twenty points or more. But I loved it. I loved being part of the team, watching from courtside seats, cheering on my friends as they shot and scored.

One day my coach announced that he and the other coach had come up with a really great idea. They were instituting an extra quarter into the game that they were calling "fifth quarter." It was to be played before the game (which I'd like to point out means it was actually not fifth *or* a quarter), and it would involve a time for the "still-developing" players to get the chance to see playing time in a gamelike situation. At that night's game, he would pick five players that usually saw a lot of bench time, and they would get to play fifth quarter while the rest of the team warmed up and got ready for the game. And he said it with a big smile on his face like it was a good thing.

But those of us who knew we'd be on the fifth quarter team saw it as anything but exciting. Sure, we got extra playing time, but let's face it: those of us selected for fifth quarter probably weren't playing basketball because we were hoping for a college scholarship. We didn't need playing time. Or extra practice. And we bench sitters certainly didn't need to be seen getting extra playing time by the students who would certainly fill the stands for that night's game.

Not surprisingly, the coach picked me as a fifth quarter player.

And not surprisingly, I flailed around the court for my eight minutes of "special playing time," bouncing balls off my foot, shooting air balls, and looking utterly ridiculous.

At one point, I glanced up to the stands and noticed a group of boys who played on the guys' team. They were, of course, all great shooters and great dribblers and great everything—and handsome to boot—and they were pointing at me and laughing. I was mortified. Not because of my basketball abilities (I already knew they were subpar) but because I had been publicly labeled as not good enough.

That was my freshman year, and I never played basketball again.

Not because I didn't have fun and not because I didn't like being on the team, but simply because I was terrified that I'd have to face another fifth quarter. A time when I knew I'd be singled out. Laughed at. Made fun of. Separated.

I'm not still upset about this—really, I'm laughing as I write this—but at the time it felt like a really big deal. It hurt. I was embarrassed and felt like I was the only one in the world who was singled out. So as I raise my kids, I pray that I never let "special" or "different" mean "bad" or "lonely" or "not good enough to play in the real game."

Erin MacPherson

Practical Steps

I have to tell you something: I felt slightly inadequate to give you tips in this section. It's a topic that is near and dear to my heart, but it's also a topic that makes me get so teary and emotional that I can't even think straight. So when it came to giving tips, I wasn't even sure where to start.

But I have friends. (I know, I'm so blessed.) My friend Ellen Schuknecht is a literal expert on social ostracizing and bullying. She has worked as a school principal for more than thirty-five years, and in that time she has made it her priority to prevent social ostracizing and bullying in her schools. She knows how devastating they can be and has written countless articles and programs on how exactly to prevent them. Here are her tips:

1. **Teach your kids to put on a flat face.** Ellen says that most bullying or social ostracizing is a result of an insecure kid who wants to prove their worth by picking on others. (Wait! I said that earlier—score one for Kathi.) Oftentimes this bully finds power in hurting other kids, so Ellen says she teaches the kids at her school to put on what she calls a "flat face" when someone is mean or cruel or bullying—they rid their face of all emotions. Not happy, not sad, not angry. Nothing. She even has the kids practice in the mirror. She says the flat face deters bullies because they get no reaction at all, and a reaction is what they are looking for.

2. **Teach your kids how not to be a victim.** Yes, it does feel unfair that your children have to adapt to either bullying or being left out, but this is actually a really valuable life skill that will serve them well throughout their lives. It's a choice to respond with dignity rather than react in a way that gives the other party what they want. Teach your kids that their response is much more important than the bully's attacks.

3. **Teach your kids how to tell.** Oftentimes victims of bullying and social ostracizing feel like they have nowhere to turn and will just be labeled a tattletale if they tell, which would make things worse. At Ellen's school, they have a wait-and-tell policy. If a kid is being bullied or sees someone being bullied, they are supposed to put on a flat face. Then, as soon as possible when the bully is not around, they should go to a trusted adult and tell them what happened. The adult will then promise to take care of the situation in a way that doesn't further victimize the kid.

4. **Brainstorm what it means to be a good friend.** A lot of bullying happens in front of others, but bystanders never step in because they are also afraid of the bully. Ellen says she teaches her students that one kind friend can make a big difference. Remind your kid how bad it feels to be lonely or bullied, and brainstorm ideas of what they can do if they

see someone else being victimized. Maybe they could go sit by the ostracized student at lunch. Or tell an adult. Or teach the student being bullied to have a flat face. By teaching your kid how to be a good friend, you can hopefully stop another child from feeling pain and also give your child the start of a friendship that could blossom.

5. **Empower your kids to pray.** Our kids need to know that every little bit of their lives is up for prayer. Pray together and often about what is going on at school.

· · · · ·

Prayers for My Child

So do not fear, for I am with you;
　　do not be dismayed, for I am your God.
I will strengthen you and help you;
　　I will uphold you with my righteous right hand. (Isa.
　　41:10)

God, you are our great protector. I pray that you come beside my kids when they feel like they are alone in the world. Show them that you are the perfect friend, the all-loving Father, and everything they need. Uphold them in their times of loneliness with a supernatural peace.

Keep on loving one another as brothers and sisters. Do not forget to show hospitality to strangers, for by so doing some people have shown hospitality to angels without knowing it. Continue to remember those in prison as if you were together with them in prison, and those who are mistreated as if you yourselves were suffering. (Heb. 13:1–3)

Father, give my kids the strength and confidence to be loving friends even when they are facing their own loneliness. Fill their spirits with generosity and kindness so they can remember those who are hurting even when they are hurting themselves. Help them to be beacons of kindness in a cruel world.

Be strong and courageous. Do not be afraid or terrified because of them, for the LORD your God goes with you; he will never leave you nor forsake you. (Deut. 31:6)

God, I know that you will never leave or forsake me. Give my kids that same confidence. Even in their darkest hours, help them to always know that you are there and you love them for who they are.

What, then, shall we say in response to these things? If God is for us, who can be against us? (Rom. 8:31)

Sovereign Lord, you are my kids' rock. You are their salvation. You are their friend. You are their hope. And if you are standing for them, who can be against them? Fill their lonely hearts with more of you this day and every day so they know who fulfills them.

The LORD is good to those whose hope is in him,
    to the one who seeks him;
it is good to wait quietly
    for the salvation of the LORD.
It is good for a man to bear the yoke
    while he is young.

Let him sit alone in silence,
>   for the LORD has laid it on him.
Let him bury his face in the dust—
>   there may yet be hope.
Let him offer his cheek to one who would strike him,
>   and let him be filled with disgrace. (Lam. 3:25–30)

My Lord, my God, you are good to those who hope in you! I pray that my kids will turn to you in their times of great pain. I pray that they will learn to wait in silence to find the hope they have in you. Help them to seek you earnestly so they can feel the incredible depth of your love for them.

· · · · ·

Prayers for Myself

At my first defense, no one came to my support, but everyone deserted me. May it not be held against them. But the LORD stood at my side and gave me strength, so that through me the message might be fully proclaimed and all the Gentiles might hear it. And I was delivered from the lion's mouth. The LORD will rescue me from every evil attack and will bring me safely to his heavenly kingdom. To him be glory for ever and ever. (2 Tim. 4:16–18)

O God, my child feels abandoned and alone right now, and the mom in me wants to go to battle, to fight. I know you are our defender. You will deliver us from the lion's mouth and bring us to safety. Lord, give me

strength to be my child's defender in a way that honors
you and your kingdom.

———————————

All my longings lie open before you, Lord;
    my sighing is not hidden from you.
My heart pounds, my strength fails me;
    even the light has gone from my eyes.
My friends and companions avoid me because of my
wounds;
    my neighbors stay far away.
Those who want to kill me set their traps,
    those who would harm me talk of my ruin;
    all day long they scheme and lie. (Ps. 38:9–12)

O God, my heart longs for happiness for my child.
I want to dry the tears, to soothe the pain. But true
happiness and fulfillment comes only from you. Give
me the strength to comfort my child in a way that is
meaningful and directs her to you for true fulfillment.

———————————

Surely he took up our pain
    and bore our suffering,
yet we considered him punished by God,
    stricken by him, and afflicted.
But he was pierced for our transgressions,
    he was crushed for our iniquities;
the punishment that brought us peace was on him,
    and by his wounds we are healed.
We all, like sheep, have gone astray,
    each of us has turned to our own way;
and the Lord has laid on him
    the iniquity of us all. (Isa. 53:4–6)

My Savior, you know the desires of my heart and the desires of my children's hearts. You have taken our pain and replaced it with salvation. You have taken our loneliness and replaced it with hope. You have taken our iniquity and replaced it with your goodness. Lord, thank you for being the only one we need. Fill my heart with hope today.

final thoughts

I understand that picking up a book like this feels like a risky thing to do. At some point, you had to feel desperate enough to say to yourself, "My kids are not turning out according to plan." You want so much more for yourself. For your children.

Whether your plans were disrupted by factors beyond your children's control or by poor choices they made along the way, I understand the pain that comes from not being able to fix your kids—or the situation.

My hope in writing this book is that you would understand one thing at the core of your being.

You are not alone.

First, you have a God who loves you and your child more than you will ever know. My prayer for myself, for my friends, and for you is from Ephesians 3:14–21:

> For this reason I kneel before the Father, from whom every family in heaven and on earth derives its name. I pray that out of his glorious riches he may strengthen you with power through his Spirit in your inner being, so that Christ may dwell in your hearts through

faith. And I pray that you, being rooted and established in love, may have power, together with all the Lord's holy people, to grasp how wide and long and high and deep is the love of Christ, and to know this love that surpasses knowledge—that you may be filled to the measure of all the fullness of God.

Now to him who is able to do immeasurably more than all we ask or imagine, according to his power that is at work within us, to him be glory in the church and in Christ Jesus throughout all generations, for ever and ever! Amen.

It will take a lifetime to understand a fraction of God's love for us—"to grasp how wide and long and high and deep is the love of Christ." But as long as we keep reminding ourselves of God's love, as long as we keep talking about it, writing about it, and praying about it, we can live in a place where we bask in his overwhelming love each and every day.

Secondly, you are not alone because you have me and tens of thousands of other moms just like me who are going through the same situations. Yes, your details may be different, but the core is the same: we love our kids, but this is not what we hoped for them.

We are out here. You are not alone. We are going to hold each other up. When one of you is in the parental pit, we can throw in a rope because we know the way out.

Keep seeking each other out. Keep loving each other. This is a long road we are on. Let's stay together and watch out for each other.

And while there are days when it feels like nothing in your child's life is ever going to change, remember there is one thing that definitely won't: God's love for them. God is crazy about your kids and is always there for you when you have any worry or concern for them. He never tires of hearing from you. He loves them and loves you. As you wait for a miracle, rest in the knowledge that your child could not be more loved.

notes

1. Brené Brown, *The Gifts of Imperfection* (Center City, MN: Hazelden, 2010), 11.
2. bell hooks, *All About Love* (New York: HarperCollins, 2000), 13.
3. Brené Brown, *Daring Greatly* (New York: Penguin, 2012), 239.
4. Rick Warren, quoted in Elizabeth Dias, "Rick Warren Preaches First Sermon Since His Son's Suicide," *TIME*, July 28, 2013, http://swampland.time.com/2013/07/28/rick-warren-preaches-first-sermon-since-his-sons-suicide.
5. Kevin Breel, "Confessions of a Depressed Comic," http://www.kevinbreel.com/#watch-my-ted-talk.

Kathi Lipp is the author of *Praying God's Word for Your Husband*, *Praying God's Word for Your Life*, *The Husband Project*, *The Me Project*, *The Get Yourself Organized Project*, and several other books. Kathi's articles have appeared in dozens of magazines, and she is a frequent guest on Focus on the Family radio and TV. She and her husband, Roger, are the parents of four young adults in San Jose, California. Kathi shares her story at retreats, conferences, and women's events across the United States. Connect with her at www.KathiLipp.com, on Facebook at www.facebook.com/AuthorKathiLipp, or on Twitter @KathiLipp.

Meet
Kathi Lipp

Kathi Lipp is a national speaker and author who inspires women to take beneficial action steps in their personal, marital, and spiritual lives.

Connect with Kathi
KathiLipp.com

With warmth and wit, Kathi Lipp shows
you not only what a blessing it is to pray
boldly for your husband but also the
amazing differences you'll see—in him and
in yourself—as you pray in full confidence
of seeing God-sized results.

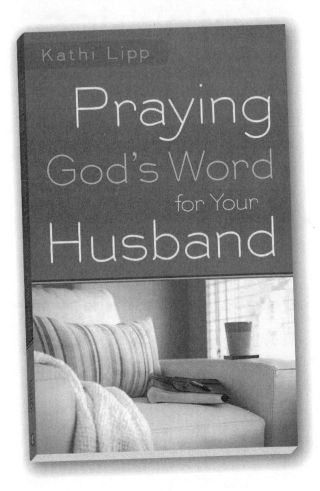

Should I pray for my own needs? Are any prayers too big or too small? Are my prayers effective? The simple strategies Kathi Lipp shares will create in women the habit of praying with renewed boldness, consistency, and expectation.

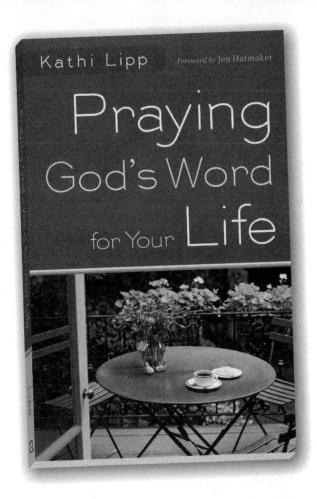